Matrimandir Talks
The Mother
1965 - 1973

AF354677

Acknowledgement

All texts are the copyright of the Sri Aurobindo Ashram Trust, Pondicherry, with the exception of the texts from Mother's Agenda.

Matrimandir Talks
Copyright : Prisma, Auroville
Author : Franz Fassbender
Photographs : John Mandeen

First edition 2021

ISBN: 978-93-95460-96-5 (Paperpack)
ISBN: 978-93-95460-70-5 (ebook)

BISAC Code:
HIS048000, HISTORY / Asia / Southeast Asia
HIS049000, HISTORY / Essays
HIS030000, HISTORY / Reference
LCO022030, LITERARY COLLECTIONS / Subjects & Themes / Places *

Thema Subject Category:
NHF, Asian history
NHTB, Social and cultural history
1FKA-IN-LG, Puducherry
JHMC, Social and cultural anthropology
QDHC2, Yoga (as a philosophy)
1FKA-IN-L, Southern India

Cataloging-in-Publication Data for this title is available from the Library of Congress.

Published by:
PRISMA, an imprint of Digital Media Initiatives
PRISMA, Aurelec / Prayogshala,
Auroville 605101, Tamil Nadu, India
www.prisma.haus

The different text fonts

Text by the Mother and Sri Aurobindo is in **Sabon normal font**

Text by the disciples: Satprem, Roger Anger, Piero Cicionesi, Huta, Shyam Sunder, Paolo Tommasi, Alain Grandcolas, Ruud Lohman and Roger Toll are in Sabon Italic font.

Gilles Guigan's words in this compilation are in Arial font.

Contents

Introduction – Matrimandir

Debashish Banerji

Sri Aurobindo and the Mother were the founders of a yoga community or ashram in Pondicherry, India, based on a system of yoga which they named integral yoga. Sri Aurobindo passed away in 1950, shortly after the end of World War II and Indian independence, so he did not live to see the enhanced phase of technology that has increasingly hegemonized the world since the mid-1960s, making industrialism, consumerism and ecological dysfunction pervasive in our times. However, the Mother lived on till 1973. In 1968, she decided to found a new international community, Auroville, in proximity to Pondicherry, which would integrate the social and political goals of Sri Aurobindo with their spiritual ideals, addressing thereby the increasing globalization of the world and the effects of global capital, and forming a model habitus for the future.

The Mother provided a charter for Auroville which emphasizes its international scope and its grounding in the effort for integration – now inclusive of psychological and cultural dimensions of the ideal of human unity:

- Auroville belongs to nobody in particular. Auroville belongs to humanity as a whole. But to live in Auroville one must be a willing servitor of the divine consciousness.

- Auroville will be the place of an unending education, of constant progress, and a youth that never ages.
- Auroville wants to be the bridge between the past and the future. Taking advantage of all discoveries from without and from within, Auroville will boldly spring towards future realisations.
- Auroville will be a site of material and spiritual researches for a living embodiment of an actual human unity.

The physical habitat of Auroville was integrated into the "integral" concerns of the city, making for a sense of "place" in the expanding identity of the inhabitants and their individual/collective yoga. This was one of several simultaneous engagements at the physical, vital, mental, psychic and spiritual levels of the collective life, forming the integral ecology and inter-related organization of Auroville as a space of collective self-determination and integral becoming.

As a community, at the center of these engagements was the idea of a city with a soul, represented architecturally by a chamber for concentration expressing solar symbolism, physically integrated through the tracking of the sun via a heliostat for focusing a ray onto a crystal globe. This structure, known as the Matrimandir (Mother's Temple), was co-designed by the Mother and French architect Roger Anger (1923-2008). The Italian Piero Cicionesi was the site architect and the site engineer. It was built by the combined labor of Auroville residents and hired help.

The present book chronicles the genesis of this structure, from idea to material form. It thus opens us to the virtual imaginary space of the

Matrimandir, where all its past and its contexts co-exist. The Mother said she saw only the Chamber. The form and the name of the structure went through a variety of stages in all its aspects. Even when the name Matrimandir was arrived at, the Mother clarified that this was not a reference to herself as a personality, but to the universal Mother. This distancing from personality may also be seen in the charter as well as in the Mother's pronouncements that Auroville should not be a place of religion. In Sri Aurobindo's philosophical vision, the term "the Mother", which he gave to Mirra Alfassa, represented the dynamic and creative Divine Consciousness, active through earth history as the evolutionary force and wisdom. The philosophical and spiritual content for this view was given by Sri Aurobindo in his text called The Mother (2012: pp. 1-26). It is the Consciousness described by this text that is behind Auroville and its soul, the Matrimandir.

A built structure at the center of the city which belongs to no single or group of resident(s) but is dedicated to their collective and integral union resonates with an archaic paradigm of temple-cities, some of which (e.g. Chidambaram) are located close to Auroville. But it resonates also with modernist experiments in Europe, by architects such as Bruno Taut, (1880-1938),who envisaged garden cities with a spiritual architectural "crown" at their center.

In its construction, the Matrimandir provided a practical focus for the fraternity, universality and anarchism coded as ideals into the charter of Auroville, as its members of diverse nationality, ethnicity, gender and class worked shoulder to shoulder, often without supervision, to give it shape. This plural painstaking effort of loving labor, sustained for thirty-seven long years of learning and working together in spiritual openness to circumstance, skill and intuition, cannot be overlooked as the process by which the vision of a collective soul was materially concretized. In keeping with the psychic aspirations of its participants, the whole magnificently exceeded by far the sum of its parts. The Matrimandir is, today, a psychic engine for the spiritual transmutation of human aspiration. Its empty, silent and vast openness, manifesting and exceeding the dreams of its builders, is its greatest strength.

It is impossible to specify the posthuman singularity of this soul of a community. Both material and metaphorical, it remains intangible in its virtuality. For all its symbolism and aesthetic taste, it is a space of concentration and nonduality. The sublime feelings evoked by it are both due to and not due to its aesthetics. Its symbolism has a deceptive plurality, in that, in its simplicity, it yet evokes an indefinable manifestation of natural and cultural echoes – womb, earth, sun, tumulus, stupa, goddess – and functions as a heterotopia due to its novelty yet repetition of familiar idea-forms. Its solar and feminine symbolism are encountered in a temporal experience (a chronotope) as one is led to a space of translucency between waking and dreaming, the inner and the outer, open-eyed and closed eyed meditation, a non-dual space at once still and radically heterogeneous, empty yet plural.

As a symbol of sustainability, it has to be noted that this experience involves centrally a metaphoric and metonymic use of the sun as a symbolic and natural source of collective life. It thus unites the space like the hub of a wheel to the totality of the community and grants it an ecological significance as part of its integral structure. It belongs to each and all of its members, its spiritual content extended individually and uniquely by each, forming the inner sustenance of their collective lives in the city. The Matrimandir is a material embodiment and constant reminder of the first tenet of Auroville's Charter, as given by the Mother: "Auroville belongs to nobody in particular. Auroville belongs to humanity as a whole. But to live in Auroville one must be a willing servitor of the divine consciousness."

Foreword

There is no record of what Mother told Udar, an engineer and disciple of the Mother (on 2.1.70 when she asked him to produce the first drawings of the Inner Chamber as per her instructions) and hardly any records of Mother's many conversations with her architect Roger Anger on Matrimandir over the years. This is very unfortunate because the conversations Mother had with these two men are far more important than those she had with Satprem and Huta.

Mother always let Roger do. She repeatedly said that she is not an architect and cannot interfere in such matters. Shyam Sunder (who was Mother's secretary for Auroville's affairs during the years 1971-73) told Gilles G. and surely others, that whenever there was a difference of opinion between Roger and some other disciples, Mother always supported Roger's point of view.

- Mother had made already two attempts to develop a new town (in 1938 for the Ashram and in 1956 for its International University Centre), which didn't manifest.

- On the first World Conference of the S.A.S. the 400 members present passed a resolution presented by Navajata (the General Secretary of the SAS) to "Develop a township near Pondicherry, with all the amenities and facilities for residence and work for those who want to prepare for a better life." But the Rules and Regulations of the SAS stipulated that "All decisions of the Executive Committee or any committee of the Society to be effective shall be submitted to the Mother for her approval and assent. No action in pursuance thereof shall be taken without the prior approval of the same by the Mother." (Mother was President of the SAS.)

- Mother's interest in this new project grew progressively and during the first half of 1965, she "took up" this township project. Early that year she named it "Auroville". In March she offered to Roger Anger, a French architect who had visited many times since 1957, and he accepted the offer.

- Two letters from an Ashram artist, Huta Hindocha, dated 20.6.65, gave her the idea of having a "Pavilion of the Universal Mother" at the centre of Auroville (instead of a house for herself as Huta had suggested to her). This seems to have enabled Her to receive her plan for Auroville.

- On 23.6.65, Mother told Satprem: "... up to now I took a very secondary interest in it because I hadn't received anything direct." (Up to now, means till receiving these 2 letters from Huta on 20.6.65)

- The Auroville Mother was speaking of at first was, physically, an extremely ambitious project.

1954

My Lord, here is Thy advice to all, for this year:
"Never boast about anything,
let your acts speak for you."

A Dream

There should be somewhere upon earth a place that no nation could claim as its sole property, a place where all human beings of good will, sincere in their aspiration, could live freely as citizens of the world, obeying one single authority, that of the supreme Truth; a place of peace, concord, harmony, where all the fighting instincts of man would be used exclusively to conquer the causes of his suffering and misery, to surmount his weakness and ignorance, to triumph over his limitations and incapacities; a place where the needs of the spirit and the care for progress would get precedence over the satisfaction of desires and passions, the seeking for pleasures and material enjoyment.

In this place, children would be able to grow and develop integrally without losing contact with their soul. Education would be given, not with a view to passing examinations and getting certificates and posts, but for enriching the existing faculties and bringing forth new ones. In this place, titles and positions would be supplanted by opportunities to serve and organise.

The needs of the body will be provided for equally in the case of each and every one. In the general organisation intellectual, moral and spiritual superiority will find expression not in the enhancement of the pleasures and powers of life but in the increase of duties and responsibilities. Artistic beauty in all forms, painting, sculpture, music, literature, will be available equally to all, the opportunity to share in the joys they bring being limited solely by each one's capacities and not by one's social or financial position.

For in this ideal place money would be no more the sovereign lord. Individual merit will have a greater importance than the value due to material wealth and social position. Work would not be there as the means of gaining one's livelihood, it would be the means whereby to express oneself, develop one's capacities and possibilities, while doing at the same time service to the whole group, which on its side would provide for each one's subsistence and for the field of his work.

In brief, it would be a place where relations between human beings, usually based almost exclusively upon competition and strife, would be replaced by relations of emulation for doing better, for collaboration, relations of real brotherhood.

The earth is certainly not ready to realise such an ideal, for mankind does not yet possess the necessary knowledge to understand and accept it or the indispensable conscious force to execute it. That is why I call it a dream.

Yet, this dream is on the way to becoming a reality. That is exactly what we are seeking to do at the Sri Aurobindo Ashram on a small scale, in proportion to our modest means. The achievement is indeed far from being perfect but it is progressive: little by little we advance towards our goal which, we hope, one day we shall be able to hold up before the world as a practical and effective means of coming out of the present chaos in order to be born into a more true, more harmonious new life.

This was first published by Mother in the Ashram Bulletin, 1954

1965

Salute to the advent of the Truth

Salute to the
advent of the Truth.

1965, June 23rd

Excerpt from a conversation with Satprem during which Mother explains to him her plan of the future town.

Have you heard of Auroville?...

Satprem: Yes.

For a long time, I had had a plan of the "ideal city", but that was during Sri Aurobindo's lifetime, with Sri Aurobindo living at its centre. Afterwards ... I was no longer interested.

Then, we took up the idea of Auroville again (I was the one who called it "Auroville"), but from the other end: instead of the formation having to find the place, it was the place that caused the formation to be born; and up to now I took a very secondary interest in it because I hadn't received anything direct.

Then that little Huta took it into her head to have a house there and have a house for me next to hers to offer me. And she wrote to me (on 20th June) all her dreams; one or two sentences suddenly awakened an old, old memory of something that had tried to manifest – a creation – when I was very small (I don't remember what age), and that had again tried to manifest at the very beginning of the century when I was with Théon. Then I had forgotten all about it. And it came back with that letter: suddenly I had my plan of Auroville. Now I have my general plan; I am waiting for Roger to make the detailed plans because since the beginning I have said, "Roger will be the architect", and I have written to Roger. ...

My plan is very simple.
It takes place up there, on the way to Madras, on top of the hill.

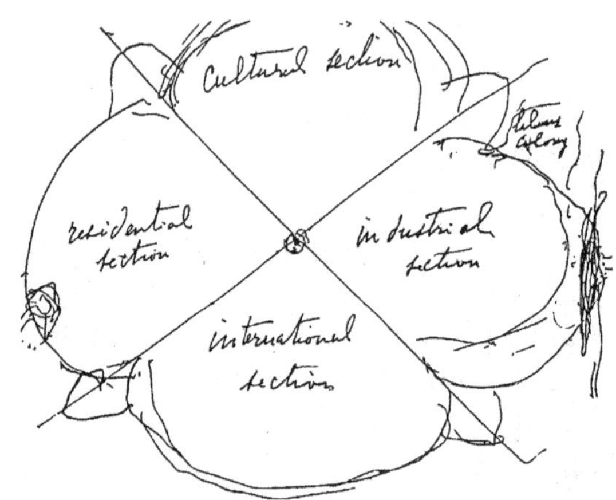

Mother's sketch of the Auroville Township

Here we have (naturally in Nature it's not like this: we'll have to adapt)
a central point. This central point is a park I had seen when I was a little
girl (perhaps the most beautiful thing in the world with regard to physical,
material Nature), a park with water and trees like all parks, and flowers,
but not too many (flowers in the form of creepers), palm trees and ferns
(all species of palm trees), water (if possible, running water – it must be
running water) and, if possible, a small waterfall – running water. From

a practical point of view, it would be very good: at the edge, outside the park, we could build reservoirs that would provide water to the residents.

So in that park I had seen the "Pavilion of Love" (but I don't like to use that word because men have turned it into something ludicrous); I am referring to the principle of divine Love. But it has been changed: it will be the "Pavilion of the Mother"; but not this (Mother points to herself): the Mother, the true Mother, the principle of the Mother. (I say "Mother" because Sri Aurobindo used the word, otherwise I would have put something else – I would have put "creative principle" or "realising principle" or ... something of that sort but it doesn't matter.)

And it will be a small building, not a big one, with just a meditation room downstairs, with columns and probably a circular shape (I say "probably" because I am leaving it for Roger to decide). Upstairs, the top floor will be a room, and the roof will be a covered terrace. Do you know the old Indian Mogul miniatures with palaces in which there are terraces and small roofs supported by columns? Do you know those old miniatures? I've had hundreds of them in my hands....

But this pavilion is very, very lovely: a small pavilion like this, with a roof over a terrace, and low walls against which there will be divans where people can sit and meditate in the open air in the evening or at night. And downstairs, at the very bottom, on the ground floor, simply a meditation room – a place with nothing in it. There would probably be, at the far end, something that would be a living light (perhaps the symbol made of living light), a constant light. Otherwise, a very calm, very silent place.

Adjoining it would be a small dwelling (well, a dwelling that would still have three floors), but not of large dimensions, and it would be the house of Huta, who would act as guardian – she would be the guardian of the pavilion (she wrote me a very nice letter, but she didn't understand all this, of course).

This is the centre. All around, there is a circular road, which isolates it from the rest. There would probably be an entrance gate (there has to be one) into the park. An entrance gate or there would be a guardian of the gate. The guardian of the gate is a new girl who has come from Africa who is Huta's cousin (to whom I gave the name Vidyota) and has written me a letter saying she wanted to be the "guardian of Auroville" to let in only the "servants of the Truth".... (Laughing) It's a very nice plan(!). So I will probably put her as guardian of the park, with a little house on the road, at the entrance... We shall see. ...

Satprem: And you will be there, in the centre?

Huta hopes so! (*Mother laughs*) I didn't say either yes or no to her, I told her, "The Lord will decide." It depends on my "health". Moving from here – no: I am here because of the Samadhi, I remain here, that's quite certain; but I can go there on a visit (it's not so far away, it takes five minutes by car). Only, Huta wants to be in peace, silence, far from the world, and it's quite possible in her park with a road around it and someone to stop people from entering – one can be really in peace – but if I am there, that's an end to it! There will be collective meditations and so on. So if I have signs (physical signs, first), then the inner command to go out, I will go there in a car and spend an hour in the afternoon – I can do it from time to time... We still have time, because it will take years before everything is ready. ...

The centre in my drawing is a symbolic centre.

But that's Huta's hope: she wants a house where she would be all alone, and next to it a house where I would be all alone – the second part is a dream because for me to be "all alone" ... you just have to see what goes on! It's a fact, isn't it, so it doesn't go well with the "all alone". Solitude must be found within, it's the only way. But on the level of life, I will certainly not go and live there, because the Samadhi is here; but I can go there on a visit. For instance, I can go for an opening or certain ceremonies – we'll have to see, it won't be for years. It's going to take years to be realised. ...

As regards the construction, it will depend on Roger's plasticity... I am not concerned about the details at all, there is only that pavilion that I would like to be very pretty – I see it. Because I saw it, I had a vision of it, so I'll try to make him understand what I saw. The park, too, I saw – those are old visions I had repeatedly. But that's not difficult.

The biggest difficulty is water, because there is no nearby river up there; but they are already trying to harness rivers. There is even a project to divert water from the Himalayas and bring it across the whole of India (Louis Allen, in-charge of the Lake Estate, an Ashram farm) had made a plan and discussed it in Delhi; of course, they objected that it would be a little costly!).

But anyway, without going into such grandiose things, something has to be done to bring water; that will be the biggest difficulty, that's what will take the longest time. As for the rest – light, power – it will be made on the spot in the industrial section – but you can't manufacture water! The Americans have given serious thought to a way of using seawater, because the earth no longer has enough drinking water for people (the water they call "fresh"... it's ironical); the amount of water is insufficient for people's use, so they have already started chemical experiments on a big scale to transform seawater and make it usable – obviously that would be the solution to the problem.

Satprem: But it already exists.

It exists, but not in a sufficient proportion.

Satprem: Yes, in Israel.

They do it in Israel? They use seawater? Obviously, that would be the solution – the sea is there. It has to be studied. Then water would have to be sent uphill.

... it will be the 'Pavilion of the Mother'; but not this.

the Mother points to herself:

The Mother, the true Mother, the principle of the Mother. I say 'Mother' because Sri Aurobindo used the word, otherwise I would have put something else – I would have put 'creative principle' or 'realising principle' or... something of that sort.

1965, June 25th

Excerpt from a conversation with Huta during which Mother explains to her plan of the future town.

Mother draws in front of Huta several sketches of Her town and gives her two out of these. She explains that Her town plan is in the shape of a flower, a hibiscus, "Godhead", to which She had recently also given the name "Auroville".

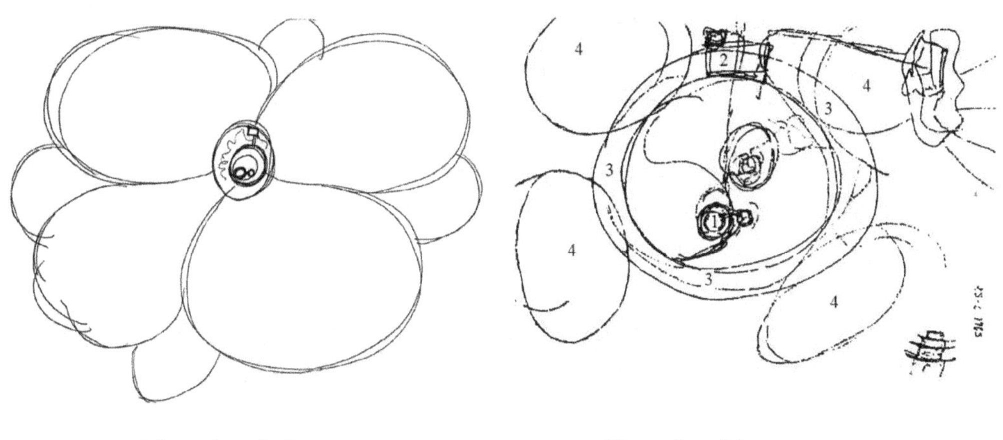

Sketch of the town   *Sketch of its centre area*

As the proper orientation of these two sketches is not mentioned, their orientation here may not be correct. Both may need to be rotated by 90° counter-clockwise.

Explanations of the reference numbers of the sketch describing the centre of the town:

The pagoda-shaped sketch (bottom right) would describe the "Pavilion of the Mother" which at that time was going to look like Kyoto's Golden Temple – except for the shape of the roof. (As Mother will tell Huta on 1.9.65.)

The two very large ovals at the centre would represent the lake. (ref. 3)

The Mother's Pavilion (ref. 1) would be on the eastern part (left) of the island. A point and two concentric circles would represent it (the two concentric circles could represent a smaller lake around it).

Huta's house would be just next to it (to its north) – represented by one circle.

The other lines on the island may represent gardens, water bodies, cascades, pathways, etc.

One has access to the island by one bridge located on the west side (ref. 2). The small rectangle at the bottom left angle of the larger rectangle represents the house of the "Guardian of the Park" (as explained to Satprem two days earlier).

The four large circular areas (ref. 4) in the four corners would represent areas planted with "huge trees". These four parks would represent the four Powers of The Mother.

The "mountain with the fir-trees" (top left) would be represented at the top left (North West), outside the lake.

After describing the main points of her sketch of the town, Mother describes its centre area:

Ah! Now, the Mother's Pavilion. This will be a separate island surrounded by a lake, tall trees, gardens with various kind of flowers.

I especially want the creepers of red hibiscus (Power) upon the outer dome of the Mother's Pavilion. They will look like living jewels against the white marble.

There will be rockeries in Japanese style, varieties of cactus, small waterfalls, small pools with lilies, lotuses, small bridges, various kinds of fountains and marble statues – one of them will be Shiva in deep trance. From his matted hair flows the water like a fountain...

There will be only one entrance. I want precious, semi-precious and artificial stones to be paved from the gate to the Mother's Pavilion in gradations, because they are full of meaning.

The Pavilion will be in white marble and will have three storeys.

The ground floor will be a huge marble hall. Nothing material is to be kept in it except an arrangement by which there will be a perpetual flame representing the Immortal Flame of the Supreme Truth.

This flame will burn in a lotus built in the centre of Sri Aurobindo's symbol and my symbol combined in a design made of pure gold. The Supreme Truth will be invoked in it.

For the second floor, I do not know yet, but on the third floor there will be a terrace garden and from this top floor the whole of Auroville will be seen.

On the terrace, I would like to have carved marble seats with satin cushions – you know marble seats – you know, they carve peacocks, flowers and things like that in marble.

The Shrine must have a vast area – not like this (*Mother takes her handkerchief in her palm and closes her hand*), so small. Also there must be a silent zone. No vehicles should move in this area, there should be no noise of any kind.

The Park of Unity will be divided into twelve gardens, which will represent the Twelve Attributes of the Supreme Mother and her Four Powers.

In these gardens, I would like to have varieties of flowers – especially the different kinds of hibiscus – the Divine Consciousness.

On the other side, towards the boundary of the gardens, I wish to have a lake, huge trees like palms, pines, various types of ferns, neem, Indian cork trees, eucalyptus and many other beautiful big trees. They all represent Unity and Aspiration.

When the lake will be dug, all the soil will be collected on one side in order to make it look like a small mountain where there will be fir trees. You see, in future there will be snow.

Beneath each tall tree around the Mother's Pavilion there would be small carved marble seats. People will meditate in the open and be one with the vastness of Mother Nature – the Mother of the multitude and Her Creation.

And you will be the guardian of the Mother's Shrine. Your tiny house in the shape of a lotus bud will be built on the island very close to my house.

Look! All these letters of yours have started the Mother's Shrine. I will explain to you more when I have spoken to the architect (Roger), who will come in September.

1965, September 1st

While looking with Huta at a photo of Kyoto's "Rokuon-ji" (Golden Temple), Mother tells her:

Child, this is exactly what we shall have except for the shape of the roof – it must be a terrace and a dome, but the surroundings will be the same – lake, flowers, trees, rockeries, small waterfalls and so on.

Ah! you know, I saw this Golden Temple at Kyoto when I was in Japan. It is beautiful.

1965, September 7th

Roger visits for the first time since his appointment as Auroville's architect, five months earlier. He brings along with him a report on the future town, which seems to be based on the description Mother made of her plan to Satprem on 23rd June, or on a very similar one.

One of Roger's recommendations is to protect the "Park of Unity" and the "Pavilion of the Mother". Roger believed he had convinced Mother to shift the centre of the town eastwards, away from the NH 32, to the area between the villages of Edayanchavadi, Kottakarai and Kuilapalayam. Mother agrees and, in addition, writes on a page of a small note-pad:

The Park of Unity must be surrounded by some kind of isolating zone so that it is solitary and silent.

One has access to it only with permission.

Le parc de l'Unité
doit être entouré
d'une sorte de
zone isolante

afin qu'il soit
solitaire et silencieux
On n'y a accès
qu'avec permission

The park of Unity must be surrounded by some kind of isolating zone

so that it is solitary and silent.

One has access to it only with permission.

1966

Let us serve the Truth.

The first record of Mother using the word "Matrimandir" dates from 7.2.68. (in an Auroville brochure). Till then, Mother referred also to it as "l'Oratoire de la Mère" in French and "The Mother's shrine" in English.
One may wonder if this word was coined by Mother, or suggested by somebody else and that Mother took some time to adopt it.

L'oratoire de la Mère

The Mother's Shrine

24. 3. 66

Message written on a birthday card,
depicting Kyoto's "Rokuon-ji" (Golden Temple), Japan,
and addressed to Roger for his 43rd birthday.

Que cette année marque le début d'une réalisation vaste et belle qui sera
le premier pas vers la Création Nouvelle.

Let this year mark the beginning
of a vast and beautiful
realisation which will be the first step towards the
New Creation.

(Mother had hoped that the construction of Auroville would start in 1966.
It would start 3 years later because it is only in January 1967 that Mother
finalised the site and in April 1968 Roger decided to start the construction
in Auromodel, where one had to start by purchasing land.)

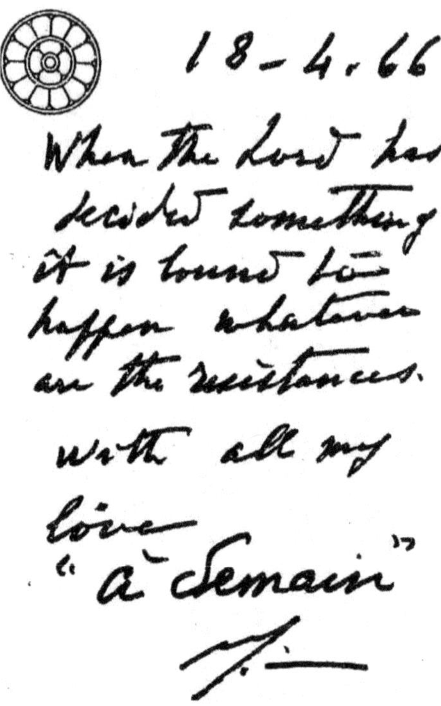

Answer to Huta who had written to know how such a large project as Auroville would be materialised without money:

When the Lord has decided something it is bound to happen whatever are the resistances.

Answer to Huta who was not very convinced about Mother's supreme vision and had expressed her feelings that everything seemed to her a dream.

My very dear little child Huta.

You say that Auroville is a dream.

Yes, it is a "Dream" of the Lord

and generally these "dreams" turn

out to be true, much more true

than the human so-called realities!

with all my love.

1967

Men, countries, continents!
The choice is imperative:
Truth or the abyss.

1967, January

Roger visits Auroville for the first time in 1967. Though, since September 1965, he believed that Mother had accepted having the centre of the town somewhere between the villages of Edayanchavadi, Kottakarai and Kuilapalayam, only very few small plots of land had been purchased in that area by the S.A.S. – and Auroville's Inauguration Ceremony should not be again postponed, which it would have to if at least some land hadn't been purchased in the future area of Matrimandir.

Roger presents to Mother a map of the area and asks Her to point on it at the centre of the future town. She points at the crossroad of two existing dirt tracks on communal lands. He and others take a jeep and drive to this place where a large and lone Banyan Tree happened to be standing. They report this fact to Mother, who feels it is a good omen and is happy about it.

As the centre of the future town is now much closer than earlier expected from the villages of Edayanchavadi and Kottakarai, Roger and his team will decide to reduce the town's diameter from 1.5km to 1.25km so that it doesn't overlap these two villages.

1967, May

Roger and 5 of his colleagues address a Press Conference in Paris, at which it is stated that work will start in Auroville in February 1968. This is the first record that (Mother had now decided that) the Inauguration Ceremony would take place during that month. The day doesn't seem to have been fixed by Mother as yet.

The Banyan tree in 1967 ▶

Excerpt from a conversation Mother has with Huta:

Ah! Now I am telling you how it will be. We want young people – teenagers – young in body and in mind.

Here we have 600 children. They will invite the children of the world. They will come with the soil of their countries. This soil will be collected in an urn of a special kind, and the urn will be sealed up.

Mother goes into a trance

The Truth Pavilion and your tiny house will be very close to each other – your house will stand between the Banyan tree and the Truth Pavilion. All these will be on an island – surrounded by water, trees and the Gardens of Unity. It will take five years if we have sufficient money. Yes... otherwise.... But I want the whole town to be built within ten years' time

Huta: Nothing is impossible for you and the Lord.

(Mother smiles sweetly) Exactly, that is what I tell people who are anxious, that the Lord will do everything. (Mother laughs softly)

1968

Remain young,
never stop striving towards
perfection

Remain young,
never stop striving towards
perfection.

1968, February 3rd

Excerpt from a conversation with Satprem:

... They wanted to make some kind of brochure on Auroville, to distribute to the press, people in the government, etc., on the 28th (Inauguration ceremony), and before that, there's a conference of all nations ("all nations" is an exaggeration, but anyway they say "all nations" in Delhi), in two or three days. And Anjani (Dayanand) is going there, and she wants to take papers on Auroville. They had prepared some texts - always lengthy, never-ending: speeches and more speeches. So I asked, I concentrated to know what should be said. And then all of a sudden Sri Aurobindo gave me a revelation. That was interesting. I concentrated to know the why, the how, etc., then all of a sudden Sri Aurobindo said...
(Mother reads a note)
   "India has become..."
It was a vision of the thing that was translated into French words right away.

«L'Inde est devenue la représentation symbolique

de toutes les difficultés de l'humanité moderne.

«L'Inde sera le lieu de sa résurrection,

la résurrection à une vie plus haute et plus vraie.»

India has become the symbol
representing all the difficulties
of modern humanity.
India will be the land of
its resurrection, the resurrection to
a higher and truer life.

And the clear vision: the same thing which in the history of the universe has made the earth the symbolic representation of the universe so as to be able to concentrate the work at one point, the same phenomenon is occurring now: India is the representation of all human difficulties on earth, and it is in India that there will be the... cure. And it is for that - it is FOR THAT that I had to create Auroville.

It came, it was so clear and tremendously powerful!

Then I wrote that. I didn't tell them how or why, but I told them: put that at the beginning of your paper, whatever it is; you can say anything you like, but this comes first. (silence) It was very interesting. It remained the whole time, for more than an hour, such a strong clear vision, as if everything were becoming clear all of a sudden. I have often asked myself the question (not "asked", but there was a straining to understand why it had become such a chaos here in India, with such sordid difficulties and all that like an accumulation), and everything became clear like that right away. It was really interesting. And then immediately it came: that's why you created Auroville. I didn't know it, you know, I was acting under pressure, and it was taking on greater and greater proportions (it's becoming really terrestrial), and I wondered why... For some time I used to think that it was the only real possibility - at present - of preventing a war, but that seemed to me a slightly superficial explanation. And then all of a sudden it came: ah, that's it!

And so, since it contained all that power, I said, "Put that". We will see - they'll understand nothing, but it doesn't matter, that will act.

Roger comes back from Paris, lands in Madras, and brings with him the model of the Galaxy, a model of its centre area and a drawing of the Amphitheatre.

First Galaxy model

Auroville's Inauguration ceremony starts at 10.30 a.m at the centre of the future town. It is attended by more than 5,000 persons and starts with Mother reading from her room at the Ashram Mother's welcoming message - in French:

28. 2. 68

Charte d'Auroville

1) Auroville n'appartient à personne en particulier. Auroville appartient à toute l'humanité dans son ensemble.

Mais pour séjourner à Auroville, il faut être le serviteur volontaire de la Conscience Divine

*

2) Auroville sera le lieu de l'éducation perpétuelle, du progrès constant et d'une jeunesse qui ne vieillit point.

3)   Auroville veut être le pont
entre le passé et l'avenir.
     Profitant de toutes les découvertes
extérieures et intérieures,
elle veut hardiment s'élancer
vers les réalisations futures.

*

4)   Auroville sera le lieu des
recherches matérielles et spirituelles
pour donner un corps vivant
à une unité humaine concrète.

Auroville Charter

1. Auroville belongs to nobody in particular. Auroville belongs to humanity as a whole. But to live in Auroville one must be a willing servitor of the Divine Consciousness.

2. Auroville will be the place of an unending education, of constant progress, and a youth that never ages.

3. Auroville wants to be the bridge between the past and the future. Taking advantage of all discoveries from without and from within, Auroville will boldly spring towards future realisations.

4. Auroville will be a site of material and spiritual researches for a living embodiment of an actual Human Unity.

28. 2. 68.

Greetings from Auroville to all men of good will

Are invited to Auroville all those who thirst for progress and aspire to a higher and truer life.

Greetings from Auroville to all men of goodwill.

Are invited to Auroville all those who thirst for progress and aspire to a

higher and truer life.

1968, February 28th
First model of the centre area of future town,
with the twelve gardens surrounding the lake.

So now, till 11:30 we have a nice quiet time like princes and kings! It doesn't often happen. If you have something to tell me I am listening.

Satprem: Maybe you are the one who has something to say?

No, no! That's enough! (Mother laughs)
I've spent all my days and all my nights quieting the atmosphere, it had taken such proportions.... You know, those movements which start whirling like that, like the wind in a cyclone or at sea, and it goes on whirling faster and faster, more and more strongly, forcefully. Then people fall ill, they get worn out, they can't do anything anymore. For the past three days I've spent my time calming and calming the atmosphere. Luckily they came to me (it wasn't to "me," naturally), they felt there was something stable here that could stop this disorder, otherwise ... But it was very difficult because of the really large number (additions from outside): on the 21st, at the Darshan, they were more than four thousand people down in the street, and there are all those who came to be here today and tomorrow, so it must mean five or six thousand people - to feed, accommodate ... whole work.

Then they asked me, naturally, that it shouldn't rain, but that it shouldn't be sunny either! (*Mother laughs*) So it was a bit difficult, but a short while ago, (name) came to tell me that Auroville's area was clouded, without sunshine.... All these little entities are quite obliging, but they're asked impossible things! I get requests, "Ah, I need rain", and at the same time, "Oh, no, I don't want rain"; "Ah, I need sunshine", and "Oh, no, I don't want sunshine...." How can they manage it!

Satprem: Are you happy?

Happy? What does that mean?

Satprem: Are things moving?

I don't know. I think they're moving all right over there.

Two days ago (name) said to me, "Oh, it has been a good lesson: now we are convinced that the Westerners' way isn't better than ours." Because they kept thinking, all of them, that the materialistic way brought about better realisations - so now they are convinced.

I told you that the Soviet consul is enthusiastic! He saw the Charter - in English first (in English, there is *Divine's Consciousness*, with the apostrophe). He said, "It's a pity, it evokes the idea of God." And Udar, who had been there (at Mother's request to convince him to attend the ceremony - and with him the entire communist block), said, "It's not that at all! There's nothing religious in all this affair. We'll show you the French." Then he read *conscience divine* (divine consciousness), and he was satisfied. He said, "This is just what we want to realise, and without these words it

1968, February 28th Frederick Buxloh together with Hero, Erisa, Renu and Austin visiting the exhibition under the Banyan tree, looking at the first design of a Matrimandir area model. The Matrimandir sphere was at this time not yet conceived and designed. ▶

would be officially recognised and supported by the Soviet government."
Then they asked him to translate it into Russian, but finally what's being
read out in Auroville isn't his translation, it's the one by T. She has just
come, and words don't frighten her. But I sent him my permission: I had it
explained to him that words were just a more or less clumsy transcription
not only of the idea, but of what is above the idea - the principle; that it
didn't matter much whether these or those words were used (each one
uses the words that suit him best), and that, therefore, I allowed him to
use the words that would be acceptable to his government. The Soviet
consul said yes, he was very glad. He said, "When the Soviet government
officially supports something, it's serious." - It's true, I know it, they are
very generous. So I hope it will have a favourable result. And you see, it's
just what I wanted: in America, for a long time they have been enthusiastic
- which is good, but perhaps they don't understand so well; the Russians,
in their nature, are mystic, and as that has been oppressed, suppressed,
naturally it has gained a lot of force. And now it tends to want to burst.

But if both together support Auroville, we won't have any more financial
hassles!

It has been coming little by little, little by little. I told you what Sri
Aurobindo revealed to me about India's condition, which was the
symbolic representation of the present condition of mankind; and that's
why, Sri Aurobindo told me, that's why Auroville has been created. Then
I understood. Since then, it has become very clear - "clear", I mean he
seems to have made it spread and people seem to begin to understand.

So there.

29th February 1968

1968, August 3rd

Excerpt from a conversation with Satprem

Though still very tired, Mother listens to a long statement on Auroville, which she rejects, and with him puts the finishing touches on a note summarising the ideal of the future city:

For thousands of years we have been developing outer means, outer instruments, outer techniques for living – and in the end those means and techniques are crushing us. The sign of the new humanity is a reversal of outlook and the understanding that inner means, inner knowledge and inner techniques can change the world and master it without crushing it.

Auroville is the place where this new way of living is being worked out, it is a centre of accelerated evolution where man must begin to change his world by means of the power of the inner spirit.

Mother then goes into a long contemplation

It seems to me to be an accelerated transformation, it's a little crushing. We'll see.

1969

No words – acts.

1969, December 18th

Mother invited Narad and Anie to develop the Garden of Unity which was to surround the Banyan tree and, like the Park of Unity would later, would consist of 12 gardens representing 12 different states of consciousness. As at that time the 12 gardens of the "Park of Unity" were to surround the Lake that was to surround the Matrimandir, these large 12 gardens couldn't possibly be developed till Matrimandir and this lake were completed. Hence the need of the Garden of Unity till the Park of Unity could be developed.

It must be a thing of great beauty, of such a beauty that when men enter the gardens, they will say, "Ah, this is it," and experience physically, concretely, the significance of each garden. In the garden of Youth, they will know youth; in the garden of Felicity, they will know felicity; in the garden of Perfection, they will know perfection and so on.

One must know how to move from consciousness to consciousness.

1969, December 31st

Excerpt from a conversation with Satprem during which he tells Mother that Paolo Tommasi and Nata feel very strongly that Matrimandir should be built at the earliest:

...I am afraid they may not even have the land. That's the difficulty, because the centre of the city has been fixed, but there's still a large part of the centre which, I believe, belongs to the government, so they're trying to negotiate so as to have it.

Roger had an idea; the idea is an island at the centre, with water around, running water which will be used for the whole water supply (of the city); and when it has flowed through the city, it will again... it will pass through... a plant, and it will go to irrigate all the cultivated lands around.

So the centre is like an islet, and at this centre, there is what we first called the "Matrimandir" – which I always see as a very large hall, absolutely bare, you understand, and getting a light from above: it should be so arranged that the light from above gets concentrated on a spot where there would be ... what we want to put as the centre of the city. At first we thought of Sri Aurobindo's symbol, but we can put whatever we want. Like that, with a ray of light constantly striking it – revolving and revolving ... (tracking the sun) you understand. If it's done well, it would be very good.

And then, below, people would be able to sit and meditate, or just rest, but there would be NOTHING – nothing except something comfortable below so they can sit without getting tired, probably with pillars acting at the same time as backrests. Something like that. That's what I always SEE. A hall (with a ceiling) high enough to allow sunlight to come in as a RAY, according to the time (of the day), and strike that centre which will be there.

If that is done, it will be very good. You could explain this to Paolo. So then, for the rest, it's the same to me, they will do as they like.

They first thought of building a dwelling for me, but I'll never go, so it's not worth the trouble, it's not worth the trouble, it's of no use at all. And to watch over the islet, it was agreed there would be a small house for Huta who wanted to be there simply as a guardian .... Then Roger had arranged a whole system of bridges to link that to the other bank. The other bank would be entirely made of gardens all around. Those gardens ... we thought of twelve gardens (dividing the distance into twelve), twelve gardens with each of them concentrated on one thing: a state of consciousness with the flowers representing it. And the twelve... (Mother corrects herself) "the last" garden would be on the islet, around (not around but beside) of this thing (the Mandir) with the tree, the banyan which is there. That's what is at the centre of the city. And there, there would be an organisation, a repetition of the twelve gardens around, with the flowers arranged in the same way...

There are now two Americans here, husband and wife (Richard & Anie Eggenberger), and he studied for more than a year in... over there, to know the art of gardening, and he came here with that knowledge. So I asked him to start straight away preparing the plan for the inner garden (that on the Island beside the banyan tree) and they're working on it.

And so, it would be enough... (But then,) the answer is always the same: "We have no money!"

Satprem: But Mother, what I think, and what Paolo too has put his finger on, is that if these ... say, twenty or fifty Aurovilians sincerely unite their hearts in the construction of this pyramid or temple of the new world, it will ATTRACT money, the millions.

It should.

Satprem: It will come. What's needed isn't to "look for millions," it's first to unite the consciousnesses around something.

Yes.

Satprem: That's the key to the millions.

You'll explain to Paolo … You remember all that I have said? …. That way we would have something really very fine.

But of course, what's needed … There are material difficulties: for this islet, we need water – naturally, otherwise it's not an islet! To have the water, we must transform it – there isn't enough underground water.

Satprem: There isn't enough water?

There is water, but it's enough for one or two houses, anyway not enough to create a permanent flow. We would need transformed sea water. In Israel they have found a way to do it economically (we even have brochures on this), economically… but you understand, economical for a city, not economical for an individual! So then, we'd need to have water to make this islet, that's the difficulty.

Satprem: But before building the islet, we can begin building the "temple", the "temple" itself … One has to start by lifting a pebble.

Yes, we could do that.

Satprem: That's the important point, it's for people to take a first pebble in their hands, put it there, and unite in that – because they'll never unite through their huts and little stories.

Yes, that would be much better.

Satprem: Oh, yes, certainly!

Naturally, logically, or psychologically rather, it's an error to build around first, and the centre afterwards.

Satprem: Of course! Of course!

How to make him understand that? ...

Satprem: Since we want to create "something else," the least we can do is to trust something else.

Yes. I'll speak to Roger about it tomorrow and I'll ask him to speak about it... to meet Paolo and see with him. I think that to a certain extent, Paolo can help bring in some money, if he is interested.

Silence

Yes. That is, to build (it) even before it's an islet.

Satprem: yes.

Silence

For the outside of this sort of temple, Roger had thought of a big lotus. But then, the inside, this play of light, I don't know whether it will be possible with a lotus shape?

If the two of them could collaborate ... If they came together and one of them were always here – one of them, now one, now another, so there would always be one of the two here – with a single plan made by them, things would go much faster, a hundred times faster.

Satprem: And this, this would seize people's hearts. That's what is required.

Yes.

I don't know... This idea of a ray of sunlight ... whenever I look, that's what I immediately see. A ray of sunlight that could come at all times of the day – it would be so arranged... (gesture following the sun's movement). And there would be something there (at the centre), which would be at the same time upright, so as to be seen all around, and lying flat, so as to receive the full light – what would it be? ... And let it not become a religion, for heaven's sake!

Satprem: Yes

... That the Force is now at work is without a shadow of doubt. And there is such a great ... (how can I put it?) it is a very active will: NO RELIGION, no religion, no religious forms. Quite naturally, people immediately ... So that's why I have left them very free. This thing... That was why I didn't insist on building the centre first, because that's in fact the cathedral of old, the temple of old, the whole thing of old (Mother makes a gesture of taking firm root), and then everything gets organised around that: a religion – we want NO religion.

1970

The world is preparing
for a big change.

Will you help?

The world is preparing
for a big change.
Will you help?

1970, January 1st

Entry in Roger's Note

Today I want to tell you something about Auroville.

Since some time I have clearly before my eyes the vision of the centre. There is a large covered area with four columns, quite high, lit from above by openings through which the light enters corresponding to each hour of the day. This vision keeps on coming since quite some time now, it is the thing to be carried out in the very first place; money will come only when this has been built. It would be sufficient if we could just build the interior – the outside after. Inside there would be nothing except the rays of light converging onto something very simple – no furniture.

There would be no windows; the light coming from above through openings corresponding to each hour of the day. A large covered area would be sufficient, with nothing on the floor.

Voilà, will you reflect on it?

1970, January 2nd

Mother has a clear vision of Matrimandir's Inner Chamber.

1970, January 3rd

Excerpts from Mother's second conversation on Matrimandir with Satprem – in which she describes to him her vision of Matrimandir's Inner Chamber.

Satprem: Mother, I told Paolo to come. You had told me to bring him. He is waiting outside.

Yes.... There is an interesting thing.

For a long time I had been feeling something, then we spoke about it (4 days ago), and... I told Roger about it, I asked him to see Paolo, and I also told him that I had seen what should be done. Naturally, he didn't say no, he said yes to everything, but I felt he wasn't too keen.... But here is what happened. I clearly saw – very, very distinctly saw, which means it was like that, and it still IS like that, it's there (*gesture showing an eternal plane*) – the inside of that place (the Matrimandir).

Satprem: Maybe you should tell Paolo about it?

Tell him right now?... All right.... I'll speak more easily if I am alone with you.

Satprem: Fine, then tell, sweet Mother.

I could describe it. It came like this. It will be a kind of hall which will be like the inside of a column. No windows. Ventilation will be artificial, with these things there (Mother points to an air conditioner), and just a roof. And the sun (beam); or, when there is no sunlight (at night or on overcast days), electric spotlight. The idea is to build right now an example or a "model" for a hundred people or so. Once the city is built and the experiment is made, we will make a BIG thing of it – but then it will be very big, for one or two thousand people. And the second one will be built around the first, which means that the first will go only when the second is built.

There's the idea.

Only, in order to tell Paolo about it (and if possible, if I see it's possible, to tell Roger about it), I wanted to have a plan. I'll have it made – not myself, I can't do it anymore; I could have done it in the past, but now I don't see clearly enough. This afternoon, I'll have it made in front of me, and then, with that plan, I'll be able to explain really well. But to you I simply wanted to say (what I have seen)....

It will be a tower with twelve facets – each facet representing one month of the year – and the top, the roof of the tower will be like this and then like that.

Mother makes a gesture showing something like this:

Then, inside, there will be twelve columns – the walls and twelve columns – and right in the middle, on the floor, my symbol, with above it four symbols of Sri Aurobindo joining in like this, to form a square, and above it ... a globe. A globe, if possible made of a transparent substance, with or without a light inside, but the sun will have to strike this globe; so, depending on the particular month or the time, it will be from here or there or there ... (*gesture showing the sun's course*). Do you understand? There will always be an opening (in the roof) with a sunbeam. Not a diffused light, but a beam that has to strike (the globe). That requires technical knowledge for its execution, and that's why I want to make a drawing together with an engineer.

But inside, there will be neither windows nor lights, it will always be in a sort of clear half-light, night and day: during the day with sunlight, at night with artificial light. And on the ground, nothing, except for a floor like this one (in Mother's room), that is, first a wooden floor (wooden or something else), then a sort of thick rubber foam, very soft, and then a carpet. A carpet covering everything, except for the centre. And people will be able to sit anywhere. The twelve columns are for those who need a backrest!

But then, people will not come for "regular meditations" or anything (of the kind) (the internal organisation will be taken care of later): it will be a place for concentration. Not everyone will (be allowed in); there will be a time of the week or the day (I don't know) when visitors will be allowed in, but without mixture. There will be a specific time or a specific day to show (the visitors), and the rest of the time only for those who are ... serious – serious, sincere, who truly want to learn to concentrate.

So I think that's good.

It was there (gesture of vision above), I still see it when I talk about it – I SEE. As I see it, it's very beautiful, really very beautiful. ... A sort of half-light: one can see, but it's VERY peaceful, and with very clear and strong light beams (the projected light, the artificial light will have to be slightly golden, it shouldn't be cold – it will depend on the spotlight). A globe that will be made of plastic or ... I don't know.

Satprem: Crystal?

If possible, yes. For the smaller (temple), the globe won't need to be very big: if it were this big (*about one foot*), it would be enough. But for the bigger temple, it will have to be big.

Satprem: But how will the bigger (temple) be built? Over the small one?

No, no, the small one will go.

Satprem: Oh, it will go, another one will be built.

But the big temple will be built afterwards, and then on a huge scale.... The smaller one will go only once the bigger one is built. But of course, for the city to be completed, we must allow some twenty years (for everything to be in order, in its place).

It's the same with the gardens: all the gardens that are being prepared are for now, but in twenty years, all that will have to be on another scale; then it will have to be something really ... really beautiful.

And I wonder what substance that globe should be made of, the big one?... The small one could be made of crystal: for a globe this size (*gesture of about 30cm*) I think it will do. One should be able to see the globe from every corner of the hall.

Satprem: It shouldn't be too high above the floor either, should it?

No, Sri Aurobindo's symbol doesn't have to be very big, it has to be this size....

Satprem: twenty-five, thirty centimetres?

At the most, at the very most.

Satprem: So it would be more or less at eye level.

At eye level, yes, that's right.
   And a VERY peaceful atmosphere. And NOTHING, nothing but big columns... It remains to be seen whether the columns would be columns of a style ... whether they will be round, or they too with twelve facets ...
   But TWELVE columns.

Satprem: And a roof with two slopes?

Yes, a roof with two slopes so as to get the sun (beam).
   It will have to be so arranged that rainwater can't get in. Something that needs to be opened and closed every time it rains won't do, it's not possible; it will have to be in such a way that rainwater can't get in. But the sun, the sun must get in AS A BEAM, not diffused. Hence it (the size of the opening) has to be limited....
   It requires a clever engineer, who knows his job really well.

Satprem: When would they start?

I'd like them to start immediately, as soon as we have the plans. But there are two questions: first the plans (workers can be found), and then money... I think that with this idea of building a small sample ("small," well, it's a manner of speaking, because to hold a hundred people easily it will still have to be big enough), a small sample to begin with – and then while building the small sample we'll learn, and (we'll build) the big one when the city will be finished – that won't be right now.

I told Roger about it, and the next day he told me, "Yes, but it will take time to prepare." (I said nothing of all I've just told you, I just spoke of doing something.) Afterwards I have seen it; so I no longer need anyone to see how it should be – I know.

What's needed is an engineer more than an architect, because an architect ... It has to be as simple as possible.

Satprem: I told Paolo what you had seen, that large room, empty, without anything. This has touched him a lot. In fact he was seeing that large empty hall. He understands quite well. So "empty" simply means a shape.

But a shape ... like a tower, but ... (that's why I wanted to have a sketch to show) twelve regular (facets), and then we need a wall that's not straight, a wall slightly like this (gesture of a slight slope), I don't know if that's possible. And inside, twelve columns and then here, we'll have to find a way to capture this (sunbeam), so that at any time of the year it can get in.... It must be someone who knows (his job) well.

The roof is like this and then like that...

As for the outside ... I didn't see the outside; I didn't see it at all, I only saw the inside. I wanted to explain to Paolo once I would have the papers, it would be easier, but since you have already called him ... let him come in.

Sujata goes out and comes back with Paolo, who comes in with a garland of pink "Harmony". Mother gives him an orange hibiscus – Auroville's flower – looks at him, and starts speaking:

Since we decided to build that temple, I have seen – I have seen the inside. I have just tried to describe it to (Satprem). But in a few days I will have plans and drawings, so I'll be able to explain more clearly. Because I don't know at all how the outside is, but the inside I know.

Paolo: The outside comes out of the inside.

It's a kind of tower with twelve regular facets representing the twelve months of the year, and absolutely empty.... Only, it will have to hold one to two hundred people. So, to support the roof, there would be inside (not outside, inside) twelve columns; and right at the centre, the object of concentration... And with the sun's collaboration, all year round it will have to get in AS A BEAM (not diffused: it will have to be so arranged that it can get in as beams); then, according to the time of the day and the month of the year, the beam will revolve (there will be some device at the top) and it will be directed onto the centre. At the centre, there will be the symbol (of the Mother), then Sri Aurobindo's symbol supporting a globe. A globe which we'll try to have made of a transparent substance such as crystal or ... A large globe. Then people will be let in order to concentrate – (laughing) to learn to concentrate! No fixed meditations, nothing of the sort, but they will have to be able to... to remain there in silence – in silence and concentration. This will require an organisation...

Paolo: It's very beautiful.

But the place should be absolutely ... as simple as possible. And the floor in such a way that people are comfortable, without having to think that it hurts here or there!

Paolo: It's very beautiful.

And in the middle, on the floor, my symbol. At the centre of my symbol, we'll have in four parts (like a square), four symbols of Sri Aurobindo, upright, and these symbols upright, like this, supporting a transparent globe.

This has been seen.

So I'll have small plans prepared by an engineer, have simple plans prepared to show, and then I'll show you when they are ready.

There. And we'll see.

As far as the walls are concerned, they will probably have to be in 'concrete'.

Paolo: The entire structure can be in reinforced concrete.

The roof will probably have to be sloping, and at the centre there will have to be a special device for the sun.

Satprem: You said that you saw the walls slightly sloped.

Inside, nothing. Nothing but the columns. The columns ... I don't know, we'll have to see if they will be with facets (like the whole thing), twelve facets, or simply round.

Paolo: Round.

Or simply square – it is to be seen.

Then, on the floor, we'll have something thick and soft. Here ... (are you comfortable when you are seated?... Yes?), there is first a wooden floor, then that sort of rubber.

Satprem: A "Dunlopillo".

Dunlopillo. Yes, that's it! And above it a woollen carpet.

Satprem: With your symbol?

Ah! The symbol will be above it.

Satprem: It will be a carpet with your symbol.

Not on the carpet. The symbol, I first thought it should be done out of some solid material.

Paolo: It has to be in stone... or in some metal.

The symbol ... everything will be around it, of course. The symbol will not cover everything, it will only be at the centre of the space – (laughing) people shouldn't sit on the symbol!... It will be in the middle.

Paolo: The room will be rather large?

Oh, yes, it should be. There should be a sort of half-light with those sunbeams – the sunbeam should be SEEN.

A sunbeam.

So, depending on the time of the day (the time of the day and the month of the year)... (the sun will go round). And then, at night, as soon as the sun disappears, we'll switch on spotlights which will have the same effect and the same colour. Night and day the light will remain there. But no windows or lamps or things of the sort – nothing. Ventilation through air conditioners (they're set inside the walls, that's very easy).

And SILENCE. No talking inside!

Mother laughs

It will be fine.

So as soon as my papers are ready, I'll call you to show them to you.

Paolo: Very good.

(Speaking to Sujata:) Give me a rose for him.

Mother gives two red roses, Paolo withdraws.

I didn't ask him if he had seen Roger because ... Roger is quite in nowadays a "practical" atmosphere.

It's good, it has to start off! It's good!

That's what I have learned, religions: the bankruptcy of religions was because they were divided – they wanted you to be like this, to the exclusion of all others. And all human knowledge have gone bankrupt because they were exclusive. And man has gone bankrupt because he was exclusive. What the New Consciousness wants (it is on this that it insists): no more divisions. To be capable of understanding the extreme spiritual, the extreme material, and to find ... to find the meeting point where ... it becomes a true force. And this is trying to teach that to the body too, through the most radical means. ...

On a practical level, I'll try to make Roger understand. But I have seen, it seems to me that what is needed is that ... when Roger is here, he looks after "Auromodel", the practical side, all that (it's very necessary, it's very good), but for this construction of the Centre, I'd like Paolo to do it, and so I'd like Paolo to stay here when Roger is gone: let Paolo be here when Roger is away, and with Paolo we would do that. Only, I don't want either of them to feel that it's one against the other(!). They must understand that it's to complement each other.

Satprem: But this, Paolo will understand it...

I believe Paolo will understand.

Satprem: But how... Roger will take it as an encroachment on his responsibilities?

Maybe not, I'll try. I'll try.

No, when I told him that it was necessary – that I have seen it and it had to be done – he didn't object. Only he told me, "But it will take time." I said, "No, it has to be done right now." And then, that's why I am getting those kinds of sketches made by an engineer, so as to show him, because it's not the job of an architect: it's the job of an engineer, with precise calculations for the sunlight, very precise, very precise. It has to be someone really skilled.

The architect will have to see that the columns are beautiful, the walls are beautiful, the proportions are accurate – all that is quite all right – and also that thing at the centre. The aspect of beauty is for the architect to see, naturally, but the whole aspect of calculations ...

And the important thing is the play of the sun on the Centre. Because it becomes a symbol – the symbol of the future realisation.

Later that day, Mother calls Udar and describes to him her vision of the Inner Chamber. He takes notes and goes to his house where he draws it as described by her. He then goes back to her room on the same day and hands her his drawing and notes.

To do this work Udar starts by making 3 drawings on two sheets of drawing paper.

1. An elevation (scale 1:50)

2. A plan in (horizontal) section (scale 1:50) together with "Sri Aurobindo's symbol cube with globe" (scale 1:5).

He then redraws these two drawings on tracing paper, from which Paolo seems to have been given a blueprint.

Matrimandir Elevation (Scale 1:50)

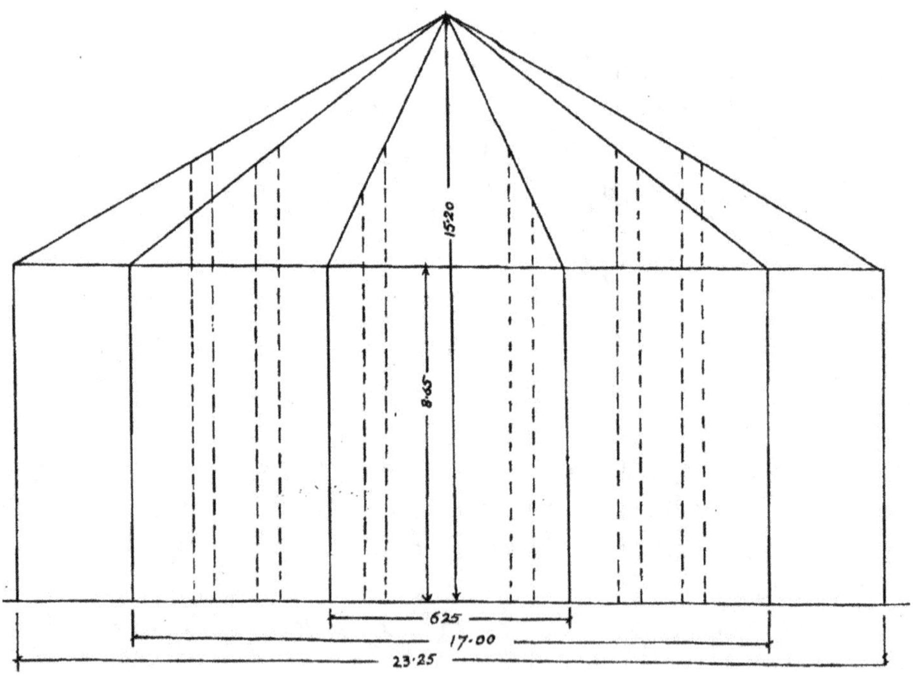

Matrimandir Plan in Section (Scale 1:50)

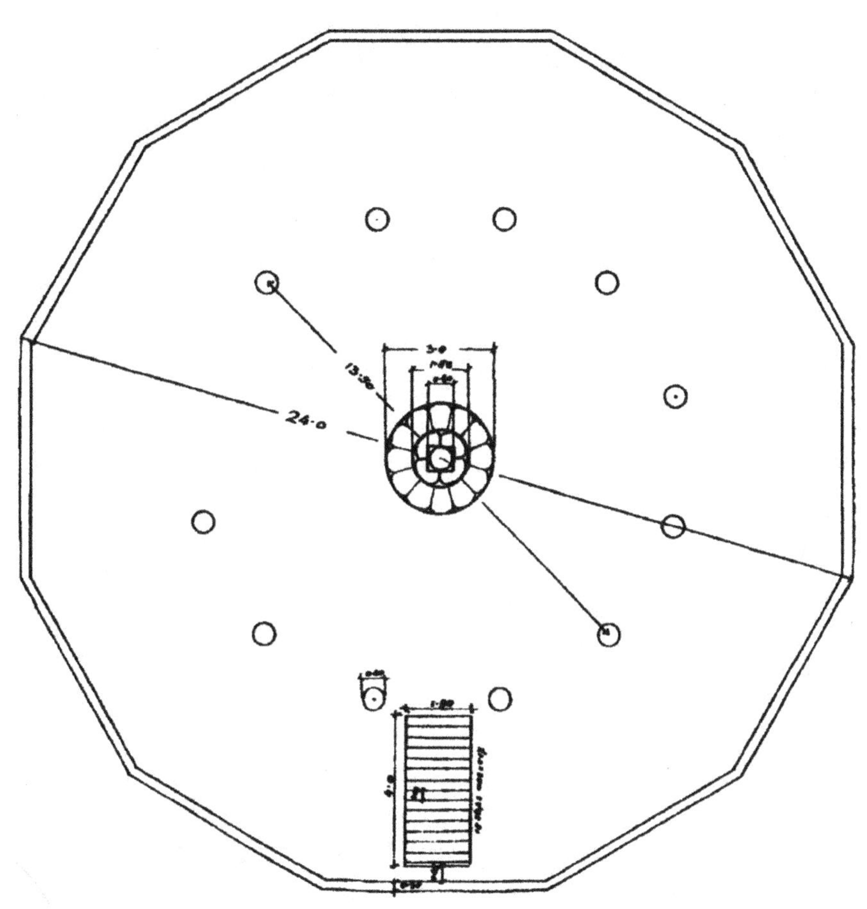

You see, this is what I have learned; the failure of religions is because they were divided. They wanted people to be religious to the exclusion of the other religions, and every branch of knowledge has been a failure because it was exclusive. And what the new consciousness wants – it is on this that it insists – is: no more divisions. To be able to understand the spiritual extreme, the material extreme, and to find the meeting point, the point where that becomes a real force.

⌒

1970, January 10th

Excerpt from a third conversation Mother had with Satprem on Matrimandir. She shows him the plans of the Inner Chamber made by Udar and explains them to him.

Satprem: I have a letter from Paolo, which I didn't read to you the other day....

I am going to see him this afternoon, Paolo, so it would be better...

Did I tell you that I saw the central construction of Auroville....? I have a plan. Would you like to see it?... Here, there are some scrolls there – one scroll. (Mother unrolls the plan while explaining it.)

There will be twelve facets. It's a circle. And, at an equal distance from the centre, twelve columns. At the centre, on the floor, like this, my symbol, and at the centre of my symbol there are four symbols of Sri Aurobindo, upright, forming a square. And atop the square, a translucent globe (we don't yet know what substance it will be made of).

Then, from the top of the roof, when the sun shines, the sun will fall on this (nowhere else, only there); when there is no sunlight, electric spotlights will send beams (again, beams, not a diffuse light) only on this, on this globe.

Then, no doors, but ... after going deep down one climbs back within... one goes under the wall and climbs back inside – it's again a symbol. Everything is symbolical.

And then, no furniture, but there is, on the floor (like here), first wood (probably) then over the wood, a thick "dunlop", and over it, a carpet, like here. We have to choose the colour. The whole thing will be white. I am not sure if Sri Aurobindo's symbols will be white ... I don't think so. I don't know it. I didn't see them white, I saw them with an indefinable colour, between gold and orange. A colour of that sort. They will stand upright, carved in stone. And a globe which is not transparent but translucent. Then, at the bottom (below the globe), a light will be projected upward and will enter the globe diffusely. And from outside, rays of light will fall.... No other lights: no windows, electric ventilation. And no furniture, nothing. A place ... to try and find one's consciousness.

Outside, it will be something like this (Mother unrolls another plan).... We don't know if the roof will have a pointed shape or... Very simple, very simple. It will hold about two hundred people. So then, Paolo's letter?

Very sweet Mother,

I saw Roger on Sunday, he came to my room and we had lunch together. With love I arranged beautiful flowers for You and Roger. You were with us. We spoke a lot. I felt Roger like a brother.

I told him that Auroville cannot be born like any other city (urban, social, economic problems, all of them to be seen later). The starting point must be "something else". That is why we must start with the Centre. That Centre must be our lever, our fixed point, the thing we can lean on to try and leap to the other side – because it's only from the other side that we can begin to understand what Auroville should be. And that Centre must be a form manifesting in Matter the content that You can transmit to us on every plane (occult included). As for us, we should only be the open and sincere means through which you can concretise that.

Then I told him how I felt the need for all of us to approach all this while living the experience inwardly and all united – people from the East and the West – in a vast movement of love, because it is the only "concrete" possible for building "something else"....

What he says is fine.

... And that Centre can give us that love right now, because it's the love of You!

I told him that, on the practical level, we could begin with a moment of silence, gathered together, try to make a complete blank, and in that blank, with everyone's aspiration, bring down the signs for the beginning.

But all of us united and together, especially the more spiritually advanced – the Indians.

Roger agreed entirely. He said we should really do that.

Mother nods her head

I'll see Paolo this afternoon to give him this plan. Because this, this is what I saw.

We'll do it in white marble. And it is Udar who said he would go and get the marble, he knows the place.

Satprem: You mean the whole structure ...?

Yes, yes.

Satprem: But Paolo told me one thing which I felt to be correct. He said, "We'll build this Centre, we'll put all our heart and aspiration into it, into this Centre ..."

Yes, yes.

Satprem: And over the years, it will get more and more charged.

Yes.

Satprem: So this Centre should be definitive, we shouldn't remove this temple to build a larger one later on.

I said that to calm people who think we need something huge. I said, "We'll begin with this, and then we'll see," you understand. I said this, this should be there until the city is completely built, and then, afterwards we would see – afterwards we won't feel like removing it!

Because a lot of people thought of something "huge."

Satprem: But Paolo says that from an architectural standpoint, it is very possible to extend the thing from outside without touching what's already built.

Oh, yes, it's quite possible.

You see, Roger asked me, "And then, what are we going to do afterwards?" I said, "Well, we'll think about it afterwards!..." – That's the trouble, they don't know ... they don't know that one must NOT THINK. As for me, I wasn't thinking about it at all, not at all, not at all – one day, I saw it like that, as I see you. Even now, it's still so living that I only have to look and I see it. And what I saw was the Centre and the light falling on it, and then, QUITE NATURALLY, while observing, I remarked, I said, "So that's how it is." But it wasn't "thought", I didn't think, "Twelve (columns) and then twelve (facets) and then..." I didn't think any of that: I saw.

It's like those symbols of Sri Aurobindo.... It's like, when I speak of the Centre, I still see those four symbols of Sri Aurobindo joined at their angles, like this, and that colour ... strange colour ... I don't know where we'll be able to find that. It's an orange gold, very warm. And it's the only colour in the place: all the rest is white. And the globe, the globe, translucent.

Satprem: He said he would inquire right now in Italy, at Murano where they make large crystals, whether they can make, say, a one-foot globe, in crystal.

There is the dimension... it ought to be written there.

Satprem: They have big glassworks there.

Oh, they do marvellous things there.
   Isn't it mentioned, the globe, its dimensions?

Satprem: Seventy centimetres.

Its diameter.

Satprem: is all this in centimetres? Yes, seventy.

This is one metre, it is more than one metre...
   It could be hollow. It need not be solid, it could be hollow? So as not to be too heavy.

Silence

Satprem: I will tell him all you have said. I will give him... I transcribe with a typewriter all that you have said. Like this it is his brief.

He's fine, Paolo.

Satprem: Yes, Mother.

That underground passageway to enter ... People will enter some ten metres away from the wall, at the foot of the urn. The urn will mark the starting point of the descent. I'll have to choose from which direction.... Then, later on, the urn might very well be INSIDE instead of being outside this thing. So perhaps we could simply have a big wall all around, and then gardens. Between the wall and the building we will build now, we can have gardens and the urn. And that wall will have one entrance (one ordinary door or several doors). One will be able to move around in the garden. Then there will be certain conditions to be met before one is allowed to descend into the underground passage and emerge into the.... It will have to be a bit initiatory: not quite "like that," not just anyhow.

Silence

To Roger I said, "We'll see that in twenty years!" So that kept him quiet.

But the first idea was to surround that with water, to have an islet so that one has to cross the water to reach the temple. It's quite possible to have an islet...

Excerpt from a conversation with Satprem during which he presents to Mother a first set of drawings done by Paolo Tommasi and explains to Mother Paolo's intentions and questions.

Paolo has removed the walls of the Chamber but has a shell outside the gallery which surrounds the Chamber. He wants to know whether 24m is the diameter of the Chamber (here its floor) or that of the shell. Mother wants the Chamber to be surrounded by vertical walls. She doesn't want this wall to be dispensed with. She also clarifies that 24m is the Chamber's diameter and not that of the shell.

During the 1970's, when neither of these two drawings were made public, people argued about whether 24m should be from one outer corner of the Chamber's wall to the opposite outer corner (as drawn by Udar in his drawings,

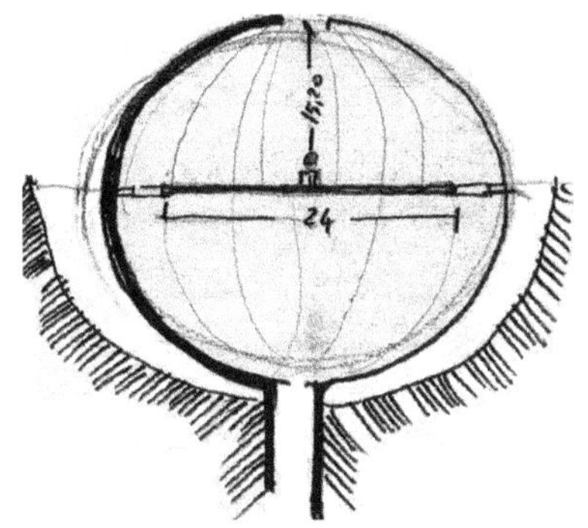

Paolo's drawing

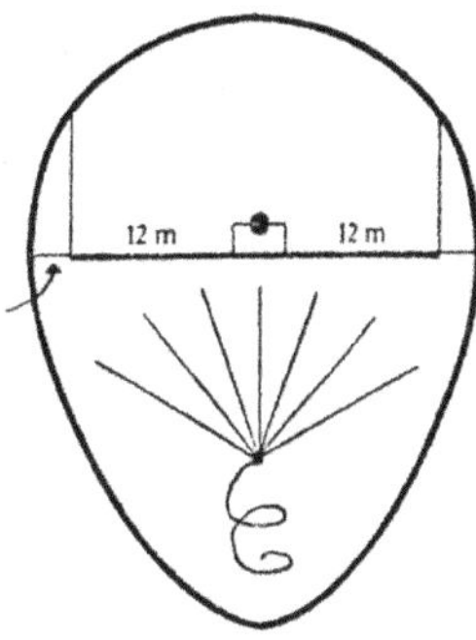

Drawing reproduced from the Agenda.
It shows what Mother means.

which had not been made public either) or from the inside of a facet of the wall to the opposite one.

This drawing was drawn on tracing paper and stuck (via scotch tape) at the bottom right of the second sheet of Paolo's drawings.

What did you want to tell me?

Satprem: I had a visit from Paolo and Nata... There are two things. But first there is the plan of the Centre – to be precise, of the outside of the Centre.

The outside, I didn't see anything. There is a sketch by Udar. I didn''t see anything at all and I am open to all proposals. So then?

Satprem: He (Paolo) explained something I found very beautiful and would like to submit to you... As a matter of fact, when you spoke of that Centre, you said, "I don't know whether the walls will have a slope or the roof." You seemed to hesitate. Then Paolo says he received a kind of inspiration and saw something very simple, like a big shell, with one part emerging above the ground and another part buried underground. He drew a sort of sketch which I'd like to show you.

Did he see Roger also? Because Roger had two ideas; he came to see me with two ideas, and I told him which of the two I liked better, but nothing is decided yet. Roger has to draw a sketch of his ideas. So I'll see that and I'll tell you his ideas.

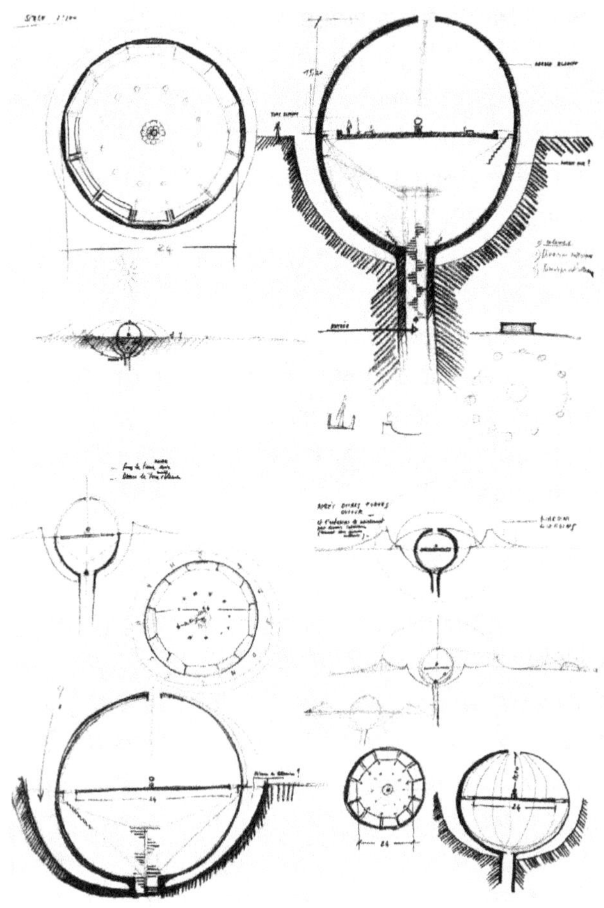

1970, January 17th
Proposals and drawings of the Inner Chamber by Paolo.

Editor's comments on Paolo's drawings:
In the drawings on the left of the top sheet, 24m is the shell's diameter while on four drawings on the bottom sheet 24m is the floor's diameter (there is a wide gap between floor and shell).

White marble is to line the inside of the upper hemisphere and black marble the inside of the lower hemisphere.

A small drawing on the top sheet show the long tunnel giving access to Matrimandir from below.

Drawings in the lower sheet show the birth of the idea of having a crater around Matrimandir. Later that year, Roger will divide this crater into 12 segments of crater and call them "petals".

The drawing in the bottom right corner of the bottom sheet is on tracing paper and taped to the bottom sheet.

(Satprem describes to Mother the drawing on the right on the top sheet.)

Satprem: So you see, this is the outside, which would simply be like a shell. The inside is exactly as you saw it: that big bare carpet, and the ball at the centre. What determined Paolo's inspiration is that you said one would have to go underground and then to re-emerge inside. So he had the idea of going deep down through a spiral staircase here, which would climb back up again, and once here, there would be a series of staircases fanning out in every direction (in the lower part of the shell) and ending inside the temple itself." Then, the whole lower part would be in black marble and the higher part would be in simple white marble. The whole thing is like a big lotus, you see, as if growing out of the earth.

Are you sure that he hasn't seen Roger? Because Roger told me, "I want to make a big circle; the inside is exactly a semicircle and the other semicircle would be underground." He told me almost the same words.

Satprem: Paolo told him his own idea.

Ah! Paolo told him! Ah, that's why.

Satprem: It's like a bud coming out of the earth.

Yes, yes, that's the first idea Roger told me, almost identically with the same words. And his second idea was a pyramid: leave the temple as we said and have a pyramid. But I also thought of a pyramid and I told him, "I thought of a pyramid...." He said he would make the two plans and we would see. But if he agrees with Paolo's idea, it's very good.

Satprem: But Roger's idea is in fact Paolo's idea.

Yes, that's right.

Satprem: So, when one reaches the top of the "stem", there are a number of staircases in every direction, so that one can emerge into the temple on any side... The centre is absolutely bare, and all around is a sort of footbridge where one emerges from the depths: that's where all those staircases end. And everything bare. There will just be that big carpet bordered from corner to corner by kinds of footbridges. It will appear to be hanging. All white and smooth. Then there was the question of the twelve columns: Paolo said he felt the twelve columns were still an ancient symbol that wouldn't go very well with the shell, and instead he suggested to have symbolically twelve supports, twelve bases of columns that would act as back rests.

Oh, but the columns serve a purpose, because atop the columns we will have spotlights to light up the Centre: there will be light day and night; during the day we'll manage the opening, but once the sun is gone, we'll turn the spotlights on, and from atop the twelve columns their rays will converge onto the Centre.

Satprem: But Mother, if the purpose of the columns is only for the spotlights, those could also be fixed on the walls?

The columns aren't near the wall, they are here, just halfway...

Satprem: Because he saw that space in the centre all bare, with just the symbol at the Centre and that big smooth carpet, without any break caused by the columns. But instead big blocks – twelve big blocks – signalling the place of the columns and also acting as supports. Twelve big blocks about 50 cm high.

It makes no sense.

Satprem: A symbolic sense? Because you did mention those pillars acting also as backrest for people who would want to sit.

Oh, for their backs.

Satprem: So he said that each of those twelve blocks could, for example, be in a different matter, as a symbol: twelve different materials.

On the outer walls we'll organise the general ventilation, which will be electrical (without windows), and atop the columns, there was the light – I saw the columns, I can't say. I clearly saw the columns.

Satprem: Well then, I'll tell him.

As for the gallery all around, I don't know that I like it a lot... I didn't see it: I saw the walls bare, without windows, also the columns, and then the Centre. I am sure of that because I saw it, and saw it for a long time.

Satprem: Does the shape of a shell suit you?

In the sense that it makes a perfect circle: half above, half below.... That's all right. Only, we'll need to arrange something for the sun.

Satprem: Yes, Nata is familiar with the problem of lighting with prisms, because to catch a sunbeam, we'll need prisms. He said he would solve the problem quite easily, he is looking into it. A few prisms will simply be put at a number of places, and they'll catch just one sunbeam.

There must be ONE beam. I SAW the beam.

Satprem: That's right, with a prism the beam will be seen. Then there will be a number of geometrical openings to follow the motion of the sun... But inside, on the wall, the twelve facets will be reproduced.

Yes, yes.

Satprem: And this (Satprem points to the circular gallery), was in principle the entrance points where one emerges from underground.

I don't know if it's good to multiply the entrance points like that.... There will be a practical problem to be solved: if there is a single entrance with a very severe watch there, it is all right, but if there are several entrance points and not enough light, there will be catastrophes.

Satprem: No, no, Mother, outside there will be a single entrance, but when one reaches the base of the shell and climbs up again, there would be that multiplicity of entrance points. Outside, there is only one way down, which ends here, at the foot of this spiral staircase.

Silence

Satprem: He thought of this footbridge all around because he said the all-white carpet at the centre would stand out better, as if floating separated, instead of being stuck to the wall.

I did not think it would be "stuck to the wall", there was always a space to circulate around the wall.

Satprem: So that's the space, with a number of footbridges on which people would emerge. And that idea of bareness was also what made him remove the columns.

What I don't like is the idea of footbridges, because the walls were straight from top to bottom, in white marble.

Satprem: Oh, but the footbridges aren't high; they are about 20 cm above ground.

Then it's all right.

Satprem: Besides, he said the carpet could come up at an angle, cover at an angle those footbridges, or rather this circulation all around.

That's quite all right.

Silence

All right, then. So they have to agree. But it must be half done already, since Roger told me about the idea. If I had known it was Paolo's idea, I would have said yes straight away. But it will be worked out. It's all right.

Satprem: So I'll tell him to work on that basis... The only question that remains is the outside: should a void be left around the shell to make the descent of the shell clearly visible? Otherwise, if the gap is filled up, it will simply look like a hemisphere placed on the ground. For the shell's descent underground to be clearly understood, he thought there would be an opening all around.

I don't know. I told you, I haven't seen anything for the outside, so I don't know. But that will be dangerous. People might fall.

Satprem: Or else we could have a sort of moat with water all around, transparent water that would make the descent of the shell clear, for instance?

Yes, yes, that could be fine.

Satprem: There is also a question of measurements. According to the plan (made by Udar), you gave 24 metres – 12 metres on each side of the globe. But could some more distance be kept for the outer circle? The plan has 24m in diameter, and 15.20 metres in height.

Oh?

Satprem: Paolo asks whether these proportions could vary: keep 24 metres for the base of the carpet, but with the possibility, for example, of keeping 2 or 3 metres on each side for passages.

Where would the walls be then?

Satprem: The wall would be here.

Satprem points to the outer side of the circular passage.

It's the walls that should be 24 metres apart.

Satprem: He says that if those passages are to be there, 24 metres wouldn't be quite sufficient.

Silence

Satprem: The height, too, is in question.

The question was in fact that it should be a perfect circle.

Satprem: If it's a perfect circle, then the height should be half the distance between the walls.

Yes.

What would really please me is if they could agree with each other and present me with a project of the two together. That way, it would be easy to execute... I mean, if Roger has adopted Paolo's idea, why couldn't they see together how to execute it?

Satprem: Yes, that would make things simpler.

Oh, much, much simpler!

What will happen under there?... (Mother points to the underground part of the shell) All that is mental. When you are going to have a big dark underground, what's going to happen in there?.. What's going to happen? – Lots of unspeakable things. Humanity isn't transformed, we shouldn't forget that! And all kinds of people will come.... Even if there is a control at the entrance, you can't stop people from going to see, and what will happen under there?... That was my first objection when Roger told me, "We could build magnificent underground passages!" I asked him, "That's very fine, but who will control what will take place under there?"

Satprem: I had thought the descent was your idea?

My idea was a rather short descent emerging here (Mother points to the only staircase from below in Udar's plan). A rather short descent, not a big underground passage like that... But it's possible; it is a question of control, that's all. Only, between an underground passage with room enough for two lines of people (one going up and the other going down) and emerging here, and a huge underground passage like this one, there is a big difference! And now he wants it all black on top of it!

Satprem: In black marble, yes.

Yes, so then? It means that one won't see very clearly. So what will take place in there?

Satprem: The underground passages aren't in the shape of narrow passageways: there is a spiral stairway, and when you reach the top of the spiral, it branches out into a series of open staircases, suspended like footbridges. It's not enclosed, it's all suspended.

Won't there be any accidents?... Oh! There's no lack of hallucinated people who might break their heads on the ground.... You see, it's a little too mental to my taste, I mean that from a mental point of view it's very attractive, but in vision...

Satprem: The idea is primarily the collective construction of this underground passage as a symbol....

Long silence

We'll see! (*Mother laughs*)

Silence

At any rate they should get together. Then I will see.

104

I'd like to have the two of them together with their paper. That would be very good.

Because the one doesn't tell me that it's the other's idea – he presents it as if it were his own(!), and then the other one doesn't tell me he spoke with the first!...

Satprem: But he didn't have an opportunity to tell you.

No, but you mentioned it because I said it to you... But I know. So you understand, we work for "human unity", and the workers don't get along!

And I clearly see, I clearly see in each one what's like this (*twisted gesture*). It's not that I am surprised, but...

My logic is this: "Yes, it's very good, you are all very nice, you work for human unity – at least be united!... Do you understand?"

Satprem: But I am sure that Paolo would be only too happy to get along with Roger.

But you surely understand that if Roger has adopted Paolo's idea, it means he admires Paolo's intelligence, otherwise he wouldn't have. So why one side like this and the other side...? We don't want any more of these petty things.

Satprem: But when Paolo showed me this plan, I felt something very beautiful... I'll tell you what I felt; I felt, I am witnessing the birth of Auroville.

No, that's not true.

Satprem: The material birth, I mean.

Yes, yes, I understand, but that's not true.

Mother goes into a long concentration

We'll let dust settle. Because, you understand, to accept those changes, I must be sure that the origin of the inspiration is of the same quality as mine... For the execution, I know very well that we need people who know the job and do the work, but for the inspiration, I must be sure that the source of inspiration is AT LEAST as high as mine... And I am not sure, because I saw so clearly. With Paolo's ideas, I saw a mixture straight away. His ideas are all mental ideas, I can assure you because for me that's very easy to see. Well, all of them bring along the same MIXTURE as with anything that's done in the world. And so... what's the use of doing over and over and over again?...

Something bothers me. Entering underground is very good, but that huge underground?...

(Mother pulls a face)

Silence

We'll see. Let it settle down, we'll see.

Satprem: And for the upper part, do we keep this idea of a shell, or should it be studied further?

Shell... The idea was a sphere. Why a shell?

Satprem: A "Shell", anyhow a round, spherical shape.

An eggshell is oblong, not spherical. The egg is really somewhat like a spinning top; so the upper part would be broader and the lower part narrower, with only the staircases... That's quite possible.

Give me a piece of paper... (Mother draws an egg while explaining) So here, all the way down, there would only be the staircases.

Like this, yes.

Satprem: His idea was to reproduce Brahman's egg – you know, the primeval egg – so that the temple would represent the primeval egg.

But then, how is it, Brahman's egg?!...

Satprem: I don't know... Like an egg, I suppose!

An egg always has its base narrower than the top. So if we conceive of an egg like this (*Mother draws*) and the base to be the staircase, a spiral staircase climbing up to the temple....

For instance, seven stairways.

Satprem: Seven instead of twelve.

And here (Mother draws a horizontal line across the "egg"), it's twenty four metres and only fifteen and a half metre high. So this way it's correct.

Satprem: Twenty-four metres for the entire width or for the carpet?

No, the walls must be straight, they cannot be curved. I saw them straight.

Satprem: Straight, and higher up rounded.

From what I had seen, the columns were higher than the walls, and that's why the roof was sloping. And it was on top of the columns that the electric lighting was placed.
    And the widest point of the egg would be here.

Mother draws a line at the level of the carpet

Satprem: At ground level.

Yes.

Satprem: And you spoke of seven openings?

Seven stairways.
    And then an underground passageway leading to the base of the egg, from where the seven stairways begin.
    That's possible.

Satprem: In other words, the inner walls of the temple should be straight.

That is, for the outside, to the eye the shape can be rounded, but inside, the wall has to be straight.

Satprem: A straight wall, and over it a dome.

Yes, a dome over the straight wall. But the dome can be the egg's dome, and I thought that the point at which the dome meets the walls would be over the columns.

Twelve columns.

And here, for the outside, they can prolong the wall in a rounded shape, like this.

Mother draws

There would even be the possibility of having a space between the outermost wall and the innermost wall. Keeping a space here. It's to be decided.

Satprem: That means, in addition to the 24 metres?

Yes, that's understood: the 24 metres end at the walls.

Satprem: And the openings for the seven stairways?

I'd rather have them outside the wall.

Satprem: Yes, it would be better because that would leave more space for the Centre.

Oh, yes, and the inside would be much clearer.   The sight of all those stairways didn't appeal to me. Even one I didn't like it, but seven... While outside, it's fine.

Satprem: So a passage outside.

The passage outside.

Satprem: Yes, as in India when you go around the temple.

Yes. So that's all right.

Satprem: And the seven stairways start directly from the base of the shell without this "stem" coming up from the bottom?

That's up to them. Below, it's the same to me. Whether they want a stairway like this or a stairway... As long as it is not too steep.

Silence

Satprem: There is the second part of the problem.

Oh, what is it?

Satprem: Nata and Paolo realised that if Auroville or the construction of this Centre is left to Auroville's people as separate from the Ashram, it will never work: the true force will never be there, those who are there aren't receptive enough to do the work. If there is that break between the Ashram and Auroville, it will never work, it will be one more "construction" but not something new. According to them, the only hope is for that Centre to be built not by Aurovilians but by all the Ashram people, without distinction between Aurovilians and non-Aurovilians; for the whole force to be united in the construction of this Centre, rather than abandon the Aurovilians to an outer break. Just as the disciples built "Golconde" (a guest-house at the Ashram), in the same way all the disciples should build Auroville's Centre, without outside manpower.

At Golconde there was outside manpower.

Satprem: Anyhow with as little as possible of the outside element, so it may be a work of consecration. Otherwise, they told me (Nata especially),

Auroville's people are all full of arrogance and incomprehension; they see the outside of things. The force of the people here should be mixed into it. If the Ashram people do not mix with them, do not breathe the force into it, it will never work.... Right now, Paolo told me, Auroville as it appears from outside looks like a necropolis.

Mother laughs

It is the "living" fruit of egoism. The only saving thing would be for the Ashram people to come in and do the work, and for the others to be absorbed in that, otherwise ...

After a long silence

But at the Ashram, we have three centres doing building work: there is Phany (Roy) who looks after the maintenance of houses, Abbay Singh, and Udar... Abbay Singh isn't equipped for that, and moreover he is too busy, because he doesn't have just building, he has all the cars and all those lands; now I consider he is fully occupied and he does his work well, so if we tried to give him too much, he couldn't do it well anymore. As for Udar, he is very interested and even said he would take care of bringing the white marble; he would himself go and choose it. He is very interested and if I told him to do it... But that wouldn't be better.

Satprem: But that's not what he meant, he didn't mean at all a problem of construction: he meant the problem of having the disciples work with the Aurovilians.... Nata, as an engineer, would look after the construction with the money collected, but the whole manpower

111

would have to be provided by all the Ashram people mingling with the Aurovilians. That's the idea.

That's not possible. All the Ashram people young enough to work are working, they all have their occupation.

Satprem: He saw a sort of rotation, each giving, for example, an hour a day, or a day a week. Because otherwise...

They'd be only too happy! For them it would be an extraordinary amusement! I have more difficulty preventing them from dissipating their energies than I would have trying to get them to do some work! For them it would be an amusement.

Satprem: Because he says that if there isn't the inner force of the Ashram people mingling with the Aurovilians, the Aurovilians will remain what they are. There is a break between Auroville and the Ashram.

As for me, I don't find it sufficient.

Satprem: The break?

Yes.

Satprem: Well, then...!

I don't find it sufficient. It's not at all on the same level. The people here...

Silence

You just have to imagine if I were gone.

112

Satprem: Bah-bah!

Just imagine that and you'll see, you'll soon see what will happen.

Satprem: Well, it's the only hope.

If they come and tell me, "YOU have to take the responsibility," ah, then I would say, "They are quite right." That's quite different. They have been beside the point. It's not that.

Satprem: But, Mother, I think that's what they mean, isn't it?

Mother laughs

They don't think clearly! It's a muddled thought.

Satprem: When they say that all the disciples here should take part in Auroville's construction, as was done for Golconde, they mean that you are the one who gives the disciples the impulse to come and participate in the work. That was the idea. But you say there should be a separation on the contrary – no mixture.

Laughing

If you knew things as they are!... Auroville people bring drugs here, they bring... all kinds of things.

Satprem: Yes, yes, I know – I know, Mother. That's why he says the only hope is...

Is for them to go and catch all those things there!

113

Satprem: He says, "Otherwise, there is no hope."

Oh no, he doesn't know! It's all in the mentality, all in the mind. They don't know. WHO knows? It's only when one sees. There isn't one who sees.

It's all thoughts and thoughts and thoughts – you can't build with thoughts.

Satprem: Can the elements in Auroville do the work?

I am working and working (*gesture of kneading*) to gather the energies that can do the work. And there has to be some sifting there.

Satprem: Yes.

Silence

But you understand, they speak of physical work, and for physical work there are only the young ones at the School – all the ashramites have become old, mon petit! They are all old. There are only the young ones at the School, and those are not here to become ashramites, they're here to be educated – it's for them to choose... Many of them, many want to go to Auroville. So that would mean the Ashram's education going to Auroville – there are many of them. But ... give me names: who can go and work with his hands?

Satprem: But, Mother, the only possibility is for you to SAY; and then, tomorrow I'll go and spend two hours in Auroville picking up baskets (of rubble)!

Mon petit, you're one of the youngest!... Can you picture me telling Nolini, "Go and work"!

Satprem: Oh, but that would pull all the others along.... Anyway, that's Nata's and Paolo's idea.

To tell Nolini (Mother laughs), poor Nolini!

Long silence

If you knew how many letters I receive from so-called Aurovilians, saying, "Oh, I want to be in peace at last, I want to come to the Ashram, I no longer want to be an Aurovilian." So there. It's just the opposite: "I want to be in peace." There you are.

Silence

As for me, you know, I don't believe in external decisions. Simply, I believe in only one thing: the force of Consciousness exerting a PRESSURE like this (crushing gesture). And the Pressure keeps increasing... Which means it's going to sift people.

Otherwise, there would be no solution, because, you see, in the past (just some ten years ago) I used to go about and see things... But that's over. It wasn't a decision I made, I didn't at all think it was over, it's not that at all: it was something that COMPELLED me. You understand? So I said all right. It's not incapacity: this body is extremely docile, it does everything it's asked to do; if it were asked to go out, it would manage

115

to go out. It's extremely docile. But that's how it is, there is a Command: NO. And I know why...

So, you know, I only believe in this: the pressure of the Consciousness. All the rest is all the things people do; they do them well or not so well, it all lives and dies and changes and gets distorted and... – all the things they've done. It's not worth it. The power of execution has to come from above, like this, imperative (gesture of descent). And for that, this (Mother points to her forehead) has to keep still. It shouldn't say, "Oh, we don't want this, oh, we want that, oh, we must do this..." – Peace, peace, peace, He knows better than you what needs to be done. There.

And as not many can understand, I don't say anything: I look and wait.

I LOOK... For instance, I am given a piece of paper as you just did when you gave me that drawing, I look like that, and I very clearly see the part in the paper that's the result from above, the part that has got mixed, the part... Like that. But you don't go and say all that!

Moreover they wouldn't believe me.

Silence

I understand very well – very well – why Sri Aurobindo didn't say "superman", why he said "supramental". He didn't say "superman" because he didn't want it to be "an improved man", that's not it. He said supramental because... He said, leave all this.

Supramental – SUPRA, you understand?

These last few days, I saw the photos of those who went to the moon.... Have you seen them? Did you see how decked out they were?

116

Satprem: Yes, I saw.

Ah ... so they've become machines.

Satprem: That's right – robots.

Yes, and then (laughing), the Russians said, "Why not send robots, it's not worth sending men!"... That's the point.

Silence

You see, Nata has spent his time speaking ill of Roger as much as he could, saying all his plans are bad and his work couldn't succeed. Roger has spent his time saying, "Nata has ruined all my work!" And another says, "This fellow ..." and this fellow says, "That fellow ..." and they are all like that! So I see in a definite way that IF the work is to be done, FIRST they have to overcome all this mean, petty humanity. They "see", they have "ideas" (they have lots of ideas), they have ideas and they see; others see other things and have other ideas, and then, "Oh, that's worthless, my idea is the right one...." They're all like that! And my whole action is like this: a PRESSURE on them to make them abdicate their little person. Until it abdicates, the work CANNOT be done.

As a matter of fact, they seek all kinds of reasons so as not to see the true one. We need ... phew, a little air!

The body – this body – is undergoing a discipline, you know, oh, terrible... But it doesn't complain, it's happy, it asks for it. And it sees how we are full of VERY SMALL THINGS that are ceaselessly hindering the action of the Force. Well, the first thing is to get rid of all that. We

117

must be like this (gesture of surrender, open) and receive the Force. Then all inspirations will come, and not only inspirations but the MEANS of execution, and the TRUE THING. Otherwise...

And since not all of them are quite ready, I do what the Consciousness does: I apply the Pressure and say nothing – I wait (Mother laughs).

Silence

If you knew all that takes place, you'd find it very funny... The whole side of agriculture, same thing; the whole side of education, same thing; everywhere the same thing... The international side, same thing: everywhere, everywhere, Man (Mother inflates her cheeks), Man puffing himself up....

FIRST they must understand: abdicate. Then we will see.

Satprem: Do I convey your message to them?

Oh, no, mon petit! Poor things, they will be terrified!

Satprem: Do you think so? It would do them good.

Oh, no, no, they'll be in a tizzy. The Pressure is the best thing. Because they don't understand what you think, they don't understand what you say: they understand what they have inside their heads. They change the meaning of the words... Like what happened with A.R. (the healer), remember how he took it as a personal attack.

Satprem: Yes, that's true! That's true, I noticed it: they take it as a personal attack.

118

Exactly. But everywhere that's the difficulty: the person first. So that spoils everything.

Satprem: You speak the truth objectively as you see it, and it's as if you were attacking them!

Attacking them, yes. So we must wait and wait till they are ripe – a lot of time is wasted, you understand. It's better not to say anything: apply the Pressure. Oh, I am pitiless! (Mother laughs a lot)

Satprem: So what do I do in the middle of all these people?

You can tell them that... In fact, Roger spoke to me (it was the same thing with other words) and I didn't say either yes or no, I was waiting because I wanted to know how others saw the thing. So now I have seen, I see that they agree. If they can agree, the work will go faster! So there. Objections of detail don't matter because you start with one idea and end with another – you progress a lot in between. So it doesn't need discussion, it's only... Only, try to put your energies together so as to start sooner, that's all! (Mother laughs)

Inspired by the oval shape of a "Shaligram" he sees on the cover of a book on "Tantra Art" by Ajit Mukherjee (first published in 1966), Roger decides to reduce the height of the sphere of Matrimandir by 20%. In a 1971 interview published in the Journal of the Institute of Indian Architects, he is quoted as saying: "It is the exact projection into space of an old tantric symbol concerning Creation and Unity". Basically, Roger understands that this shape represents the primeval egg and hence the unity of creation and he finds it very fitting to have such a shape at the centre of a town dedicated to human unity.

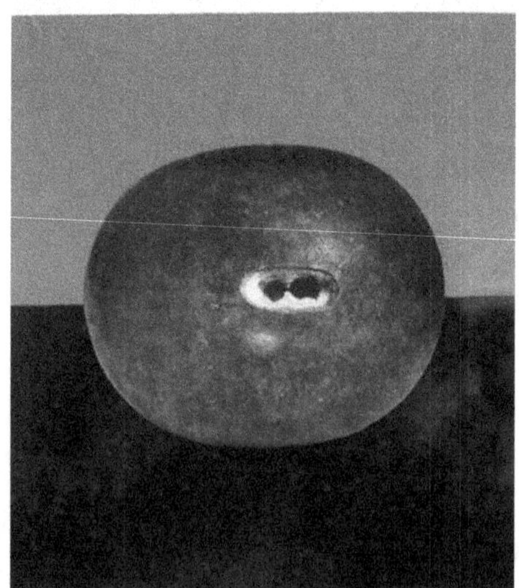

Front cover of
Ajit Mukherjee's
book on "Tantra Art"

1970, March 24th

Roger presents to Mother five models of the Matrimandir together with a half-model of its Inner Chamber. These models are seen below when exhibited at the Ashram's meditation room.

Mother comments on the three pyramidal models saying:

"One doesn't step on the Matrimandir" and opts for the above model in which an inverted brass pot represents the Matrimandir.

Matrimandir Inner Structure

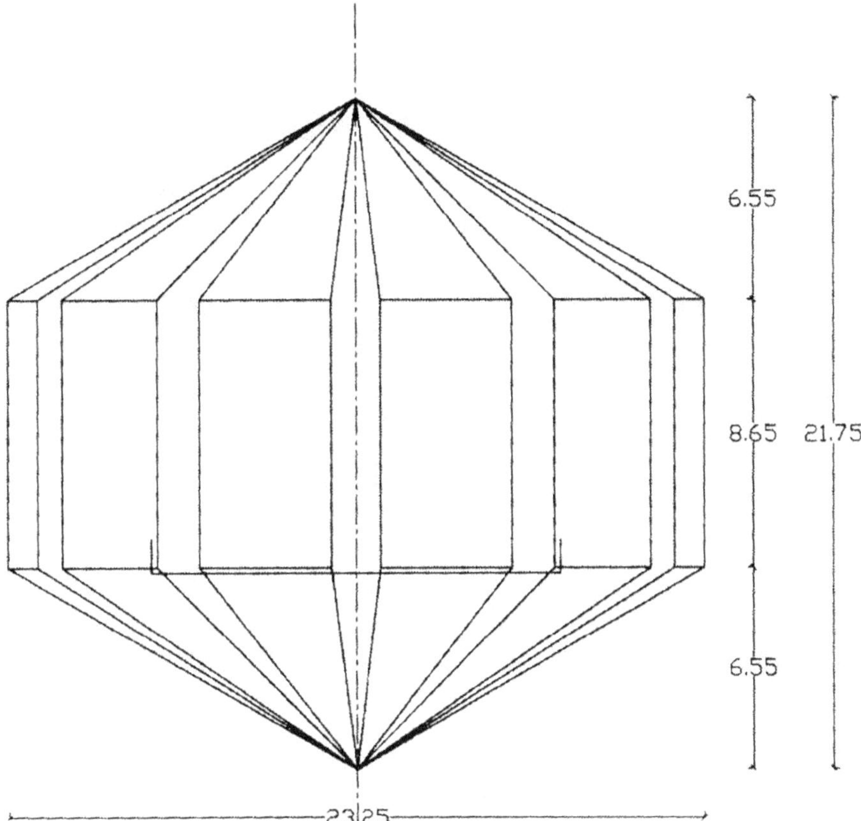

Horizontal section above the level of the Matrimandir Chamber's floor.

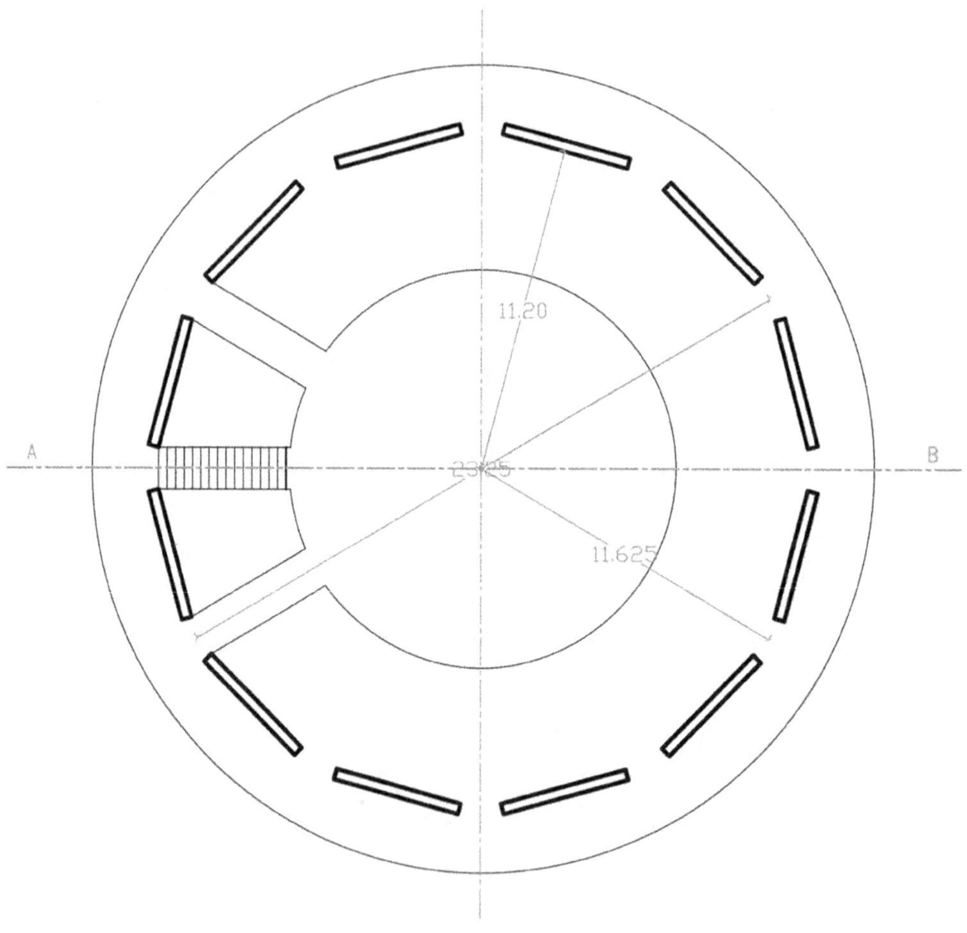

Matrimandir Inner Chamber, vertical section.

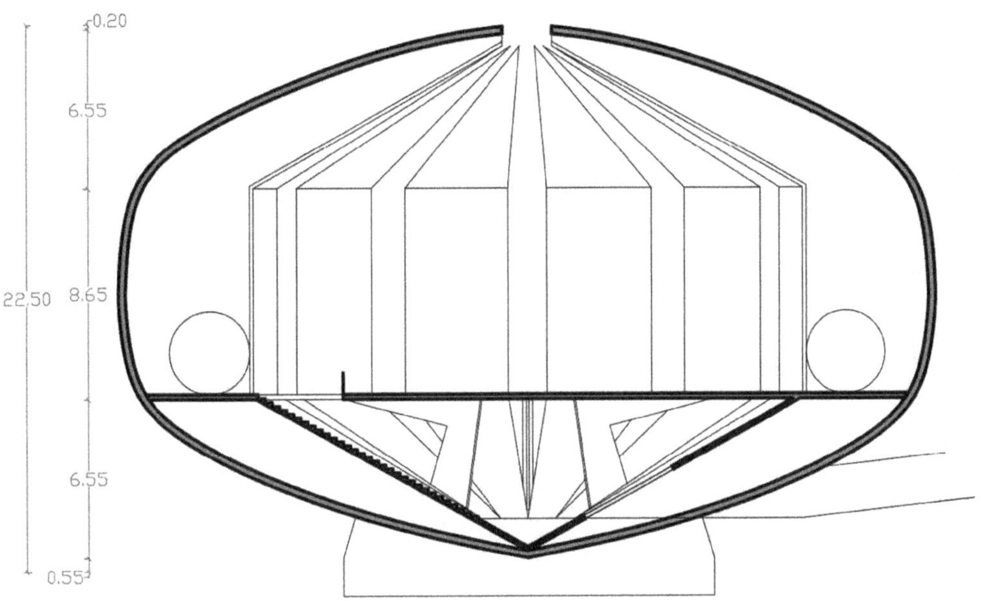

Horizontal section just below the level of the Matrimandir Chamber's floor.

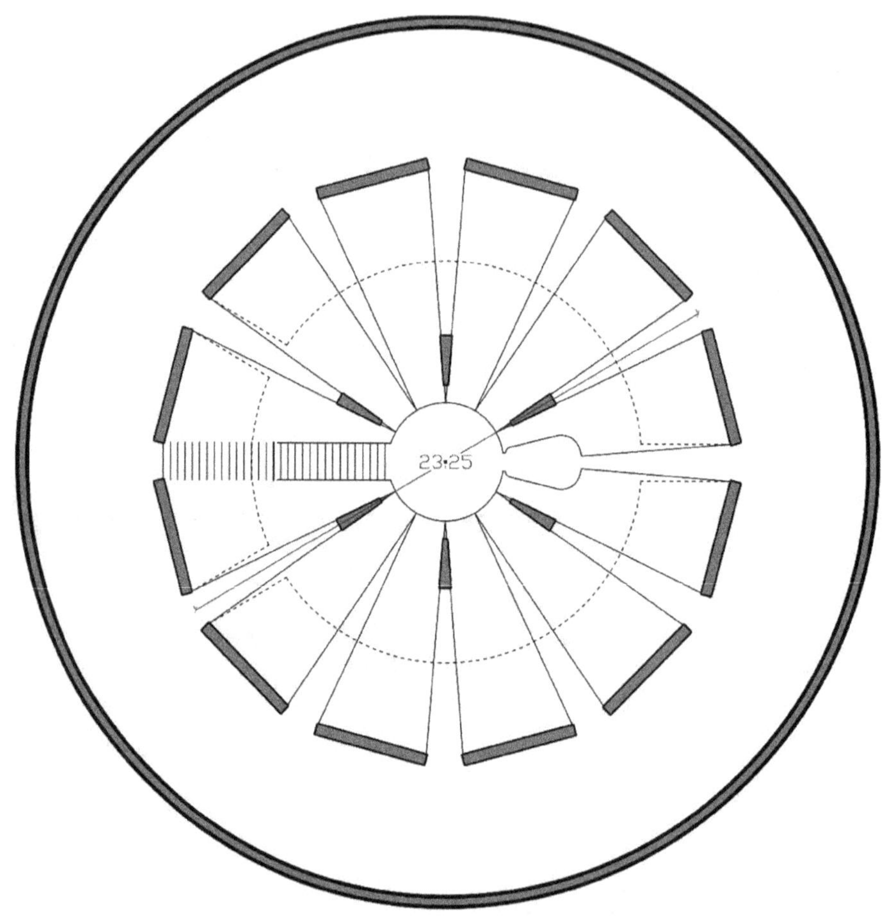

Half-model of Matrimandir's Inner Chamber

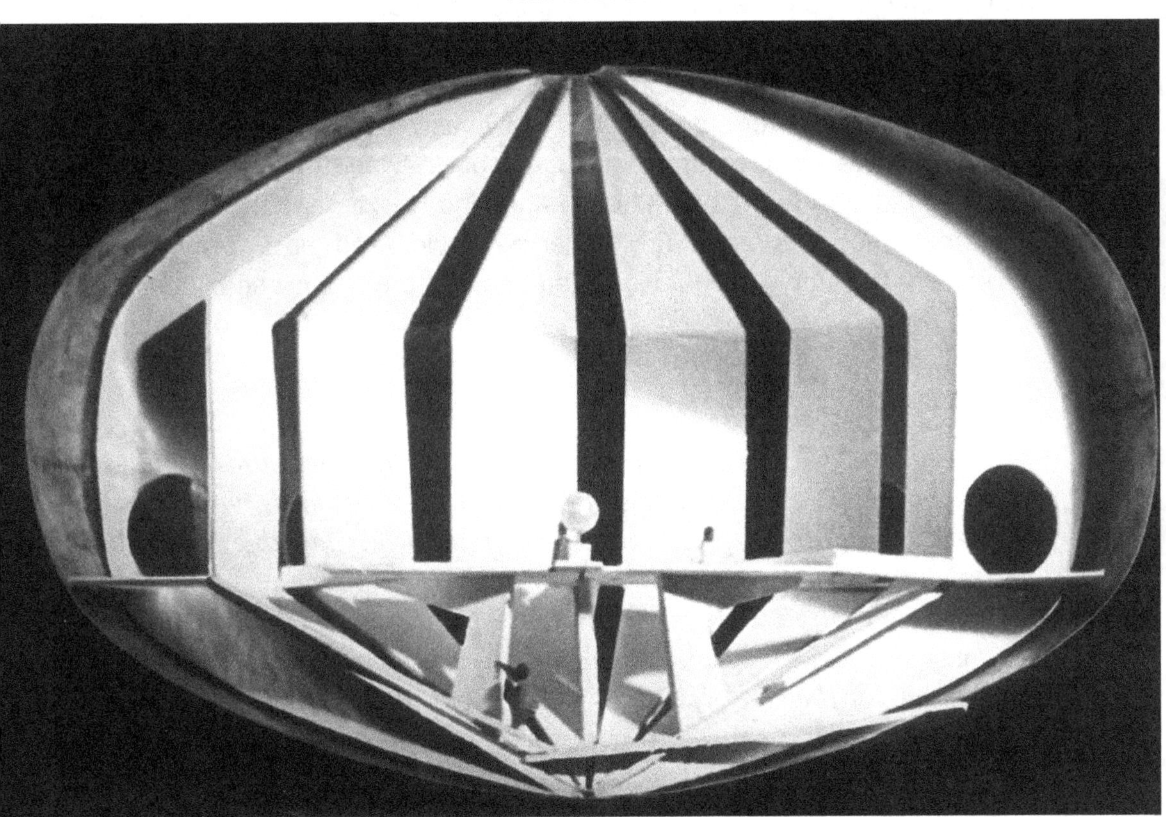

There are no columns. As was the case in Udar's drawing and in Paolo's drawing, the Chamber is accessed from below but one doesn't have to go so deep as in Paolo's concept.

As was the case in Paolo's drawings, there is a gallery all around the room and the Chamber can be accessed by gaps between the facets of the dodeca wall. This seems to mean that Roger and Paolo had agreed on this idea.

The carpet's diameter is 13.5m; hence its area is 143m2. Would it extend to the walls, it would cover some 400m2. Obviously, 200 persons won't be able to meditate there. This means that Roger wasn't aware that, on 17th January, Mother had told Satprem that the carpet needed to extend to the dodeca wall. (On 10th January, Satprem told Mother he would send the transcript of their conversations to Paolo. Roger would later say Satprem didn't send it to him.)

(Excerpt from Roger's open letter dated 20.04.77.)

On March 24, '70, I presented 5 models to Mother and a maquette presenting the lines of the interior of the hall. The columns were no longer represented in that maquette and there figured already the access to the hall by a stair-case leading to a gallery encircling the hall.

After having looked at them for long, having asked for the necessary explanations and having spent time over each of the models, Mother chose one to serve for the elaboration of the concept of the present Matrimandir and she gave me her consent for the work as a whole.

1970, March 28th

Mother dictates to Her son, André Morisset, who handwrites it:

It has been decided and remains decided that the Matri Mandir will be surrounded with water. However; water is not available just now and will be available only later. So it is decided to build the Matri Mandir now and surround it with water only later; perhaps in a few years' time.

As regards the Matrimandir itself I (Mother) have selected our plan which agrees with the vision I had of the inside and has my full approval.

Therefore there is no need to worry. The Matri Mandir will be built now and water brought round it later.

1970, May 13th

Roger asked me to say what we mean by religion...

Satprem: Sweet Mother, the notion of religion is most often linked to the search for God. Should religion be understood in this context only? As a matter of fact, are there not nowadays other forms of religion?

I wrote something down BEFORE receiving this question. It came in English.

We give the name religion to any concept of the world or the universe which is presented as the exclusive Truth in which one must have an absolute faith, generally because this Truth is declared to be the result of a revelation.

Most religions affirm the existence of a God and the rules to be followed to obey Him, but there are some Godless religions, such as socio-political organizations which, in the name of an Ideal or the State, claim the same right to be obeyed.

To seek Truth freely and to approach it freely along his own lines is a man's right. But each one must know that his discovery is good for him alone and it is not to be imposed on others.

And then this:

In Auroville, nothing belongs to anyone in particular.

Everything is collective property.

It's hard for me to talk.

Text written during the "Aspiration Talks", as distributed on this day:

Auroville and the Religions

We want the Truth.

For most men, it is what they want that they label truth. The Aurovilians must want the Truth whatever it may be.

Auroville is for those who want to live a life essentially divine but who renounce all religions whether they be ancient, modern, new or future.

It is only in experience that there can be knowledge of the Truth.

No one ought to speak of the Divine unless he has had experience of the Divine. Get experience of the Divine, then alone will you have the right to speak of it.

The objective study of religions will be a part of the historical study of the development of human consciousness.

Religions make up part of the history of mankind and it is in this guise that they will be studied at Auroville – not as beliefs to which one ought or ought not to adhere, but as part of a process in the development of human consciousness which should lead man towards his superior realisation.

PROGRAMME
Research through experience of the
Supreme Truth
A life divine but
NO RELIGIONS

Our research will not be a search effected by mystic means. It is in life itself that we wish to find the Divine. And it is through this discovery that life can really be transformed.

1970, May 24th

Answer to a question from Shyam Sunder:

For the last three days the idea has been coming that the "Matrimandir" in Auroville ought to be built soon.

It would indeed be good, and would change things in an unexpected way – but this does not seem to have been revealed to others.

1970, July 7th

Excerpt from the 8th "Aspiration talk":

Cristof reads to Mother a letter written by Rod H.:

Divine Mother, there is great confusion about Auroville's organisation, inner as well as outer. How can we work together towards the realisation of a higher consciousness? It seems that Auroville should become a more homogeneous community with a greater sense of unity.

In order to realise this, would it be possible for all the inhabitants of Promesse, Hope, Aspiration, Peace, etc, to meet in order to work together one day a week on a communal garden, perhaps the Garden of Truth?

Or each person could devote one day a week to a communal farm, to produce food for Auroville. That would help us to get to know each other better and make us more capable of organising ourselves in the right spirit. And perhaps the people engaged in individual projects for Auroville could also work together more closely, so as to form a sort of guiding team in Auroville, so that each one's work could progress more effectively.

Would such a concerted effort in Auroville just now help us to do your work?

With a prayer of perfection.

The aspiration is good, but... I don't know whether the time has come.

Cristof: He is not the only one. There are several people working in different places in Auroville who feel this need to unite and to do the same work together.

Yes, the idea is good, but this is how I see it. We want to build the Matrimandir; and then, that was the idea: when we begin to build the Matrimandir, everyone who wants to work there will be able to do so. And that would really be working on the central idea. And it should be soon. It should have been already. So there, there will be work for everyone. We have been thinking of beginning the Matrimandir for a long time. In fact, everyone should come and work there, except, of course, those who work elsewhere. There will be work for everybody. It is better than... It is the centre of the town. You could tell him this: in principle the idea is good. But as for the application, for a long time, more than a year, we have wanted to begin the Matrimandir so that everyone could work there. A person would have to say, "No, I do not want to" and have his reasons. It is like the Force, the central Force of Auroville, the cohesive Force of Auroville. There will be gardens. There will be everything, all the possibilities: engineers, architects, all kinds of manual work. So you can tell him from me that he has picked up the idea which was in the air, but that we want its application to be truly symbolic. And when we begin to build the Matrimandir, we will put everyone to work on it. Not every day and all the time, but it will be organised.

1970, August 14th

People from Auroville and the Ashram gather for a first invocation of the Matrimandir near the Banyan tree.

This function took place around a circular and shallow pond which had been built immediately south of the Banyan Tree at the time of Auroville's Inauguration Ceremony (and would later be demolished).

Mother sends this message to be inscribed by the shallow pond near the Banyan tree:

The Matrimandir wants to be the symbol of the Divine's

answer to man's aspiration for perfection.

Union with the Divine

manifesting in a progressive human unity.

People from Auroville and the Ashram gather around the shallow pond close to the Banyan tree for a Matrimandir dedication ceremony.

The Matrimandir wants to be the

symbol of the Universal Mother according

to Sri Aurobindo's teaching.

1970, November

Roger Anger is back from France where he sojourned for almost four months. He brings with him a new set of drawings for Matrimandir, which underwent there a radical transformation. It has become much higher and more complex. The simplicity Mother had originally spoken about isn't there anymore. It will thus take a lot more time and money to complete. It seems nevertheless obvious that Mother approves Roger's new plans.

Editors comments on this new concept:

Matrimandir is now covered with golden discs and is surrounded by twelve 15m high "petals" and twelve smaller petals.
As was the case in the previous concept, there are no columns.
Pillars and ribs are somehow similar to what they will be in the final concept. Matrimandir is thus much higher than in the previous concept.
Entering the Chamber is again from below (as in the case in Udar's drawing), but instead of a single staircase, there are now four, which is better in terms of symmetry but staircases and their guard-rails divide the Chamber into 4 distinct spaces. One enters the room very close to the globe which will be very disturbing for those who meditate.
There is still a gap between carpet and dodeca wall - not for a gallery but to provide headroom for spiral ramps. This means that the Chamber's seating capacity is much less than in Udar's drawings and in the final concept.
Eventually, the dodeca wall will only enclose the Chamber and there will be only one set of spiral ramps. In this concept, the dodeca wall encloses also the

space between ribs in the lower hemisphere and there are two sets of spiral ramps.

Access to the Chamber is via staircases in the pillars leading directly to the 2nd level and then via spiral ramps which are within the dodeca wall.

Exit from the Chamber is via spiral ramps which are between dodeca wall and shell and lead to the first level. From there a different set of staircases lead to the space below Matrimandir.

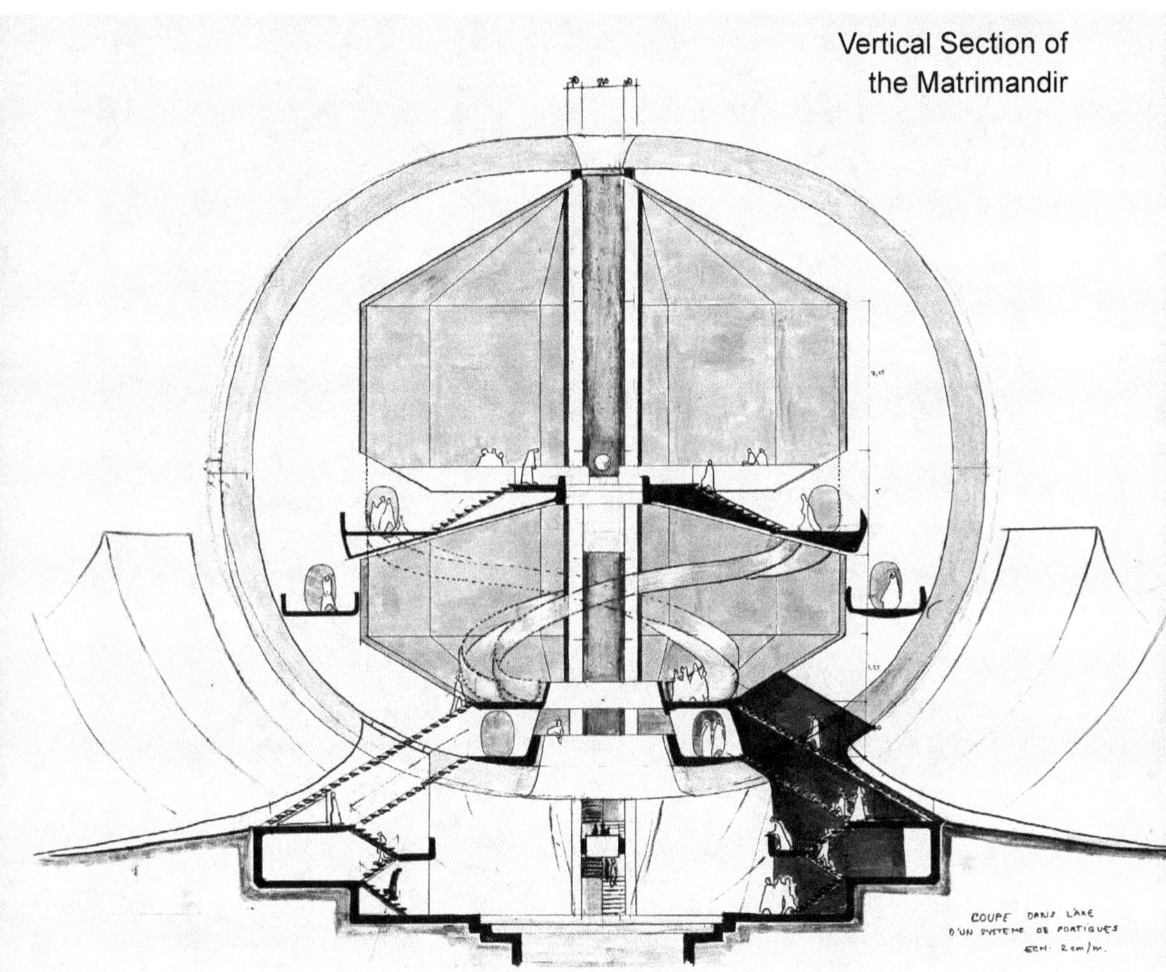
COUPE DANS L'AXE
D'UN SYSTEME DE PORTIQUES
ECH: 2cm/m.

3

Answer to Oscar, the editor of the Gazette Aurovilienne,
who had written to ask something on Matrimandir.

The Matrimandir will be the soul of Auroville.

The sooner it is there, the better it will be for everybody and especially

for the Aurovilians.

1971

*Blessed are those who
take a leap towards the Future.*

Blessed are those who
take a leap towards the Future.

1971, February 16th

Since some Aurovilians were in favour of having Matrimandir built by a contractor while others felt that "the soul of Auroville" should be built by the Aurovilians.

Shyam Sunder asked Mother.

For the construction of the Matrimandir, will only Aurovilians do the work or will there also be hired workers and other people of goodwill?

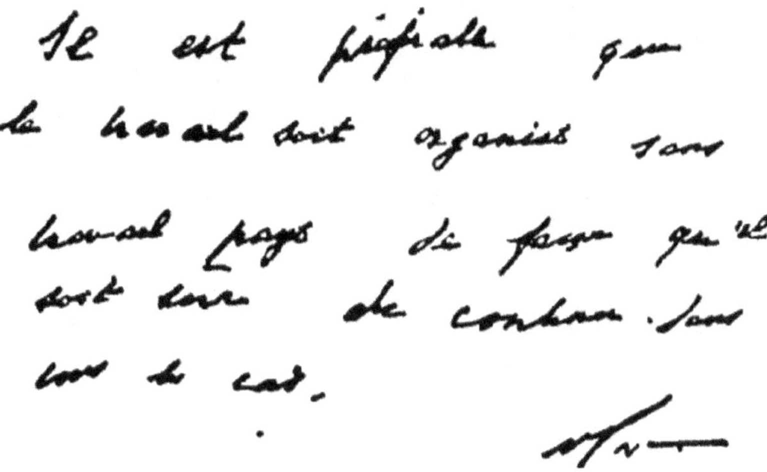

It is preferable that the work be organised without paid labour so that it
is sure to continue in all circumstances.

1971, early

The date chosen for laying Matrimandir's foundation stone is nearing but, as yet, it has not been possible to purchase the land on which it is to be built.

Entry in Roger's notes:

Can he change the position of Matrimandir? He should move his town. That's all. (movement of hand falling)

If one could move to a place where there has been no question of buying, and where people would be very happy to sell.

It is a question of decisive will... of not being attached to one's small mental combination ... We will make Auroville very close to it.

Me, I am sure that if I would drive up there by car and would see the place ... I would find a place where one could do it and where people would be happy to sell. I am sure of it.

Likely location of the Matrimandir's
first foundation stone, 21st February 1971

Matrimandir

An agreement had been signed for the purchase of the land on which Matrimandir now stands (but would only be finalized mid March), its owner allowed the construction of a 12-pillar altar on the future site of Matrimandir and a meditation to be held there – provided everything would be removed the following day. Matrimandir's foundation stone was therefore laid in the adjacent (poromboke) land outside the hole which needed to be dug for the foundations. It is now very close to Matrimandir's west radial and to the two small "petals" which border it. (In order to lay Matrimandir's first stone below its foundations, it would have been necessary to first dig a 10m deep hole in that place).

1971, February 21st

To mark this occasion, a card is distributed. It features a photo of the thermocol model of the future Matrimandir and its gardens and the following words of the Mother:

Let the Matrimandir
be the living symbol of Auroville's
aspiration for the
Divine.

Laying of Matrimandir's Foundation Stone

The function started with a meditation around a fire burning in the middle of a 12-pillared altar. It was followed by Nolini-da's reading and then by the laying of the foundation stone by Aurofilio and Nolini-da.

The Foundation stone of the Matrimandir was laid at the centre of Auroville on 21st February 1971, exactly at sunrise at 6.30am. A fire, symbol of the human aspiration, had been lit in front of a simple yet magnificent altar and the large gathering sat in a semi-circle, facing the East, while the air resounded with the Mother's message and the music.

An extract from Sri Aurobindo's book "The Mother" was read out by Nolini Kanta Gupta:

"The Mother's power and not any human endeavour and tapasya can alone rend the lid and tear the covering and shape the vessel and bring down into this world of obscurity and falsehood and death and suffering Truth and Light and Life Divine and the immortal's Ananda."

◄ A fire, symbol of man's aspiration,
was lit as the Mother's message was heard.

Le 21 Février 1971

pose de la première pierre
du Matrimandir

bénédictions

1971, February 21st
Laying of the foundation stone of
the Matrimandir.

Blessings.

The first Foundation stone of the Matrimandir was laid at sunrise at the centre of Auroville on Mother's 93rd birthday, 21st February 1971.

Navajata holding the Foundation stone,
with Roger Anger, Aurofilio and Nolini Kanta Gupta.

1971 February 21st,
first model of the Matrimandir structure.
The dodeca wall is here extended
below the equator
of the building, it is not so at present.

A page of the Matrimandir brochure, blessed by Mother.

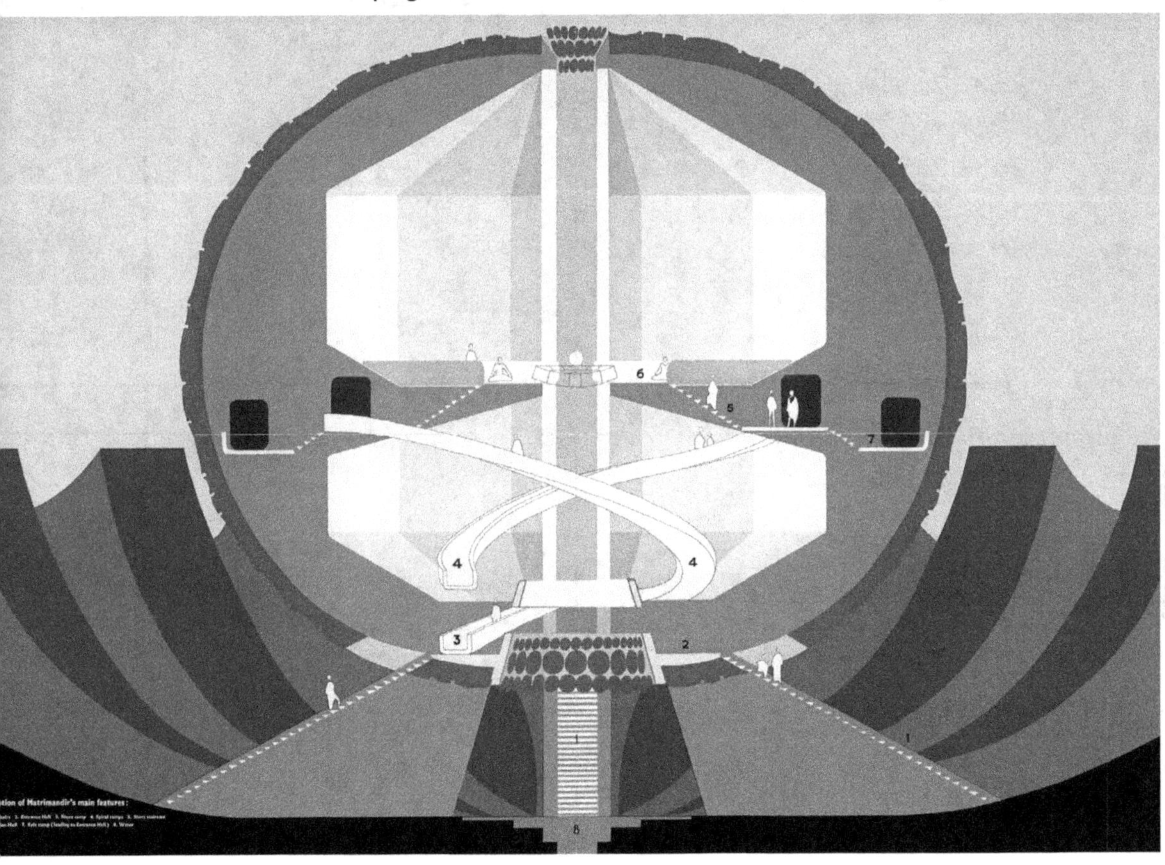

159

Answer to the Aurovilians working at the Matrimandir Nursery who had asked Mother whether they should postpone growing flowers and plants in order to join in digging the excavation for the Matrimandir:

No,

the gardens are as important
as the Matrimandir itself.

The Mother

While this was happening, a van delivered the "rosewood model" (which had just been completed); it was placed on the platform which was still surrounding the Banyan tree's trunk. A model of Matrimandir's structure was also exhibited there. Some plans and exhibition panels were also there to explain to the public Roger's latest plans for Auroville's centre area.

◀ The (rosewood) model of Matrimandir gardens was exhibited for the first time under the Banyan Tree on Mother's birthday, 21st February 1971.

1971, February 22nd

Letter from Satprem to Roger

Dear Roger,

I wanted to tell you that yesterday I had the very strong perception or sensation in front of the fire. Suddenly I felt as if an OM was springing up from the ancient times of Vedic Sacrifice and we were there to round off a whole cycle – to such an extent that when I heard Sunil's music, I was surprised as though I were hearing the hymns to Agni of the Vedas. It was extremely powerful. Something did take place yesterday. It is good for the future.

With very cordial regards.
Satprem

Mother asks Auroville's land purchaser Shyam Sundar at what time exactly he would meet the owner of the land on which Matrimandir is to be built and She instructs him to pay the price demanded.

She then writes this message:

For those who have

some land to sell.

There is a

Supreme Divinity

witness of all our

actions and the

day of the

consequence will come

soon.

The Mother

1971, March 14th

Now that the land for Matrimandir has been purchased, two months earlier, an agreement had been signed and an amount paid.
On that day Mother gives this message for the starting of the excavation of the foundation of the Matrimandir by Aurovilians, Ashramites and other friends:

The fraternity of

collaboration.

The aspiration

towards Unity

in joy and Light.

Blessings

The Mother

Excerpt from an interview of Roger published in the April/June 1971
issue of the 'Journal of the Institute of Indian Architects'.

Q. What is the Matrimandir?

R.A. As Mother has said:

"The Matrimandir wants to be the symbol of the Divine's answer to man's aspiration for perfection, the union with the Divine manifesting Himself in a progressive human unity". Here is the model. You can see how the earth opens as if it were under the pressure of an irresistible force. And the golden sphere of consciousness comes out of the depths. The spiritual meaning is obvious. It shows how out of the evolution of earth shall come the new age promised by all traditions.

Q. If I understand correctly, this is a religious building?

R.A. No. If it were, I would have designed a cathedral or a temple. The meaning of the Matrimandir is above all religions. It expresses the spiritual endeavour, itself the rebirth of man into a new consciousness – "Realisation" as it is called in India.

Q. How did you get the idea of building such a symbol?

R.A. The idea is not mine; Mother of Sri Aurobindo Ashram gave us the assignment. She told us to build the Matrimandir before other things.

She gave precise indications about the measurements and the arrangement of the main inner chamber of the Matrimandir. The measurements were precise almost to the centimetre.

Q. How could she, not being an architect, determine such exact measurements?

R.A. This I don't know, you must find the answer for yourself. Well, with the information she had given us, we started to work and evolved a general shape which is nearly spherical.

Q. You have just told us about the meaning of the Matrimandir and how the project was initiated. Would you now explain the architectural conception?

R.A. Without going into all the details, I can give you a general description. We started with many models that were shown to Mother, and She chose this one. As you see, the general shape is nearly spherical. Observe that I say nearly spherical: it is the exact projection into space of an old tantric symbol concerning Creation and Unity. When looked at from above, the building is circular and when viewed from the side, it is slightly oval. From whatever side, it keeps the same aspect.

Q. What materials have been chosen?

R.A. Inside there will be white marble and a structure in rough cast concrete. Outside, this basic structure is not covered in a final manner: we chose to leave provision for future changes so that the outer aspect of the Matrimandir may be modified according to the evolution of consciousness of Aurovilians.

In order to achieve this idea, we designed a plastic "skin" that covers the inner structure. This "skin" itself will be covered by golden discs also in plastic, fixed at the end of iron rods that will move slightly in the wind. The sunlight will be reflected on this entire moving surface and will produce a sort of vibration which seems to come from the building itself. It will give the feeling of a mass of light that is alive.

Let us now take a closer look.

First of all we come to a circular area composed of 12 gardens designed like opened lotus petals. None of these gardens is similar to the others. And yet they make up an overall design. They are separated by streams that originate at the four points of the compass. These streams delineate the shape of the 12 gardens. All together they reproduce the symbol of Mother. Separately now, they express each of the aspects of Mother through a floral decoration that may be changed according to the artistic will of the gardeners. The flowers are placed in removable vats.

After passing these gardens, we continue on one of the paths leading to the building. There are 12 paths altogether going through a landscape of pyramid-like masses of dense earth, delineated by the streams that unite the ponds of the gardens.

It takes us straight to the Matrimandir. As we go on, the earth becomes higher and higher on each side. It forms a twelve-sectioned crater from which arises the Matrimandir. Now we are walking between 2 oblique walls, 30 feet high, as impressive as a fault line. The walls become lower and lower. We are in the crater. And here is the Matrimandir. It looks as if it were suspended in the air in the middle of this strange corolla.

Before entering the structure, see a water tank under the sphere. The bottom side of the building seems to rest above the water which, though it is in the shade of the building, receives daylight directly... Let us look up: the Matrimandir is open, in the vertical axis, from top to bottom. A column of light pierces the building.

The doors to the Matrimandir are in the pillars. Walking now into the building through one of them, we climb up a staircase towards an elevated inner room. This room is a wide landing before the spiral ramp leading us further on to the main chamber.

Two spiral paths reach this chamber, 2 others lead outside; the landings of the ramps separate the area into 4 equal parts. In the centre, our eye is focused on a luminous ball – 2 feet in diameter. It receives the light coming from the top, diffuses it into the room beneath. We would like to keep this ball suspended and immobile in the air by means of a magnetic field. It is easy to understand that this main chamber is devoted to meditation.

Here is revealed the second spiritual meaning of the Matrimandir. Until now, the consciousness was emerging from the depths of matter. But there is another force, another consciousness, which is secretly similar to the first one. Yes, remember that we spoke of the light coming from above. These are two powers: one is hidden in the sacred heart of things and is at once their reason for being, their basis and their life. It is a rising force, a power that breaks open the crust of matter. But there is also a descending power that comes from the heights, from the Supreme level, a down-going force that awakens. It stimulates the emergence of an ever new creation. The conjunction, the meeting of these two forces in the heart of the Matrimandir symbolises the perfect Realisation.

Speaking of symbols, you have noticed 2 figures: 4 and 12, which come frequently in this composition. Have a look at the model. You see the shape of Mother's symbol. It is a kind of seal which is integrated into the whole project. Finally, coming back to our visit to the Matrimandir, we shall start on our way out of the main chamber by any of the 2 spiral ramps located between the concrete frame and the plastic "skin" which covers the Matrimandir like a cocoon. An opalescent light passes through the skin itself.

A last word: the road which surrounds the garden of the periphery has exactly the same shape as the Matrimandir, that is, the tantric shape we spoke about earlier. The area encircled by the road is exactly 10 times bigger than the Matrimandir's, outline. Interesting... It happened without conscious intention. Puzzled, I asked Mother about the occult signification of the number 10. She answered that 10 is the figure of accomplishment!

Excerpt from Roger's note after a conversation with Mother on Matrimandir.

In India the creation, that means basically the work of the Mother-Creator, has for centuries been considered as anti-divine. Sri Aurobindo has shown/taught that it is in Matter that the Divine must be manifested; he has insisted on the understanding of this concept of the Mother as Creator.

Matrimandir is here to teach people that it is not by escaping from the world or ignoring it that they will realise the Divine in life. Matrimandir must be the symbol of this Truth. I don't want it to be made into a religion; with all my force I refuse. We don't want dogmas, principles, ritual, absolutely not, absolutely not.

Q.: Why do we build Matrimandir?

For the great majority of Indians there is no need for an explanation; they know from their background; it is for the Westerners and the Americans of whom one in a million is able to feel that it is necessary.

Q.: Will the Force be more specially concentrated in Matrimandir?

The new Force works everywhere, especially in this room. You feel it, don't you? There is here a density capable of performing miracles, but few are able to feel it, to perceive it. Sri Aurobindo and I have concentrated this Force on the whole town; it is palpable, perceptible as a very concrete perfume which penetrates, but one must be able to feel it, to receive it. But no miracles as people would like to see; for them to believe, they need material proofs without which they deny. Build Matrimandir; put in place my symbol and Sri Aurobindo's and the suspended globe. I take it upon myself to make it into a very powerful centre. Only those who are capable will perceive it.

Message given by the Mother to help raise funds for the Matrimandir.

Donne ton argent à
l'Œuvre Divine et tu seras plus
riche que si tu le gardes.

Give your money
to the Divine work and you will be
richer than you would be by keeping it.

1971, September 21st

A student from the Centre of Education, Ranajit Gupta, who works with Piero, finalises a first set of five measured drawings of the Matrimandir. The horizontal section below (drawn above the Chamber's floor) show the Chamber's dodeca wall, the four staircases and the wide gap between the Chamber's floor and walls (in order to provide some headway to the spiral ramps). The drawing on the next page show that one accesses the Chamber via a pair of ramps located within the dodeca wall and exit it via a second pair of ramps located outside it.

Horizontal Section
of Matrimandir's
Inner Chamber

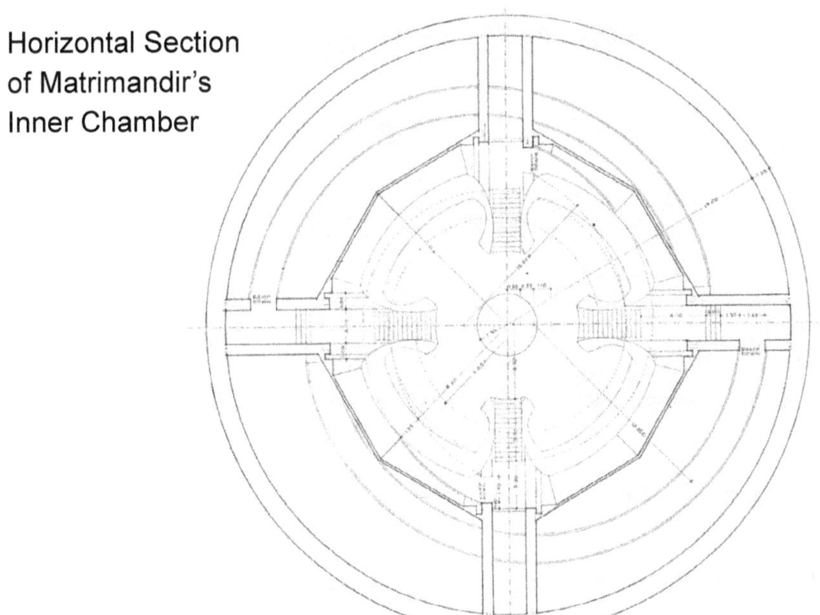

Answer to a concern:

The Matrimandir is directly under the influence of the Divine and certainly He arranges things better than we could do ourselves.

—

1971, October 5th

Having constructed a special building at their Centre, some devotees asked Mother to give her consent to their naming it "Matrimandir"; the following conversation ensued:

Champaklal: Mother, there is only one Matrimandir, the one you are building in Auroville. This name should not be used anywhere else.

Champaklal later remembered that, without his asking for it, Mother wrote the following note:

> There is only one Matrimandir,
> the Matrimandir of Auroville.
> The others must have another name.
>
> The Mother

1971, October 10th

Typed notice, drafted by Roger and signed by Mother with Blessings.

The building of the Matrimandir now requires the support of all men of goodwill, both inside and outside Auroville.

The help of specialised and qualified contractors, backed and supported by the enthusiasm and faith of the Aurovilians, is necessary for its rapid construction.

Blessings

Aurovilians and others digging the earth at site of the Matrimandir. In the beginning they had insisted to do all the work themselves. Only when this was too much time-consuming, workers from the villages were employed.

1971, November 3rd

Question from Alain Grandcolas and Mother's answer to it:

Alain: Can you give some general ideas about the way in which you want the Matrimandir to be built, so that we shall have no more doubts and may build with light and confident hearts?

Strength, safety, durability, harmonious balance.

The foundations are especially important and should be done by experts.

There is room for everyone of goodwill, and for those who in all sincerity and simplicity want to offer their work, there is enough to keep them usefully occupied.

Blessings

1971, November, as the excavation is not progressing fast enough, local workers are hired to complete the work at the earliest. There will be up to 400 of them working under the supervision of Alain Grandcolas.

1972

*Let us all try to be worthy
of Sri Aurobindo's centenary.*

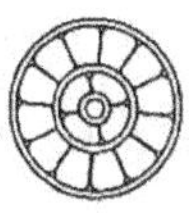

Auroville wants to be
the first realisation of human unity
based on the teaching of Sri Aurobindo,
where men of all countries would be at home.
blessings

The Mother

1972, early

Quotation from Sri Aurobindo sent by Mother to the Gazette Aurovilienne for publication in answer to a question.

It is certainly a mistake to bring down the light by force - to pull it down. The Supramental cannot be taken by storm.
   When the time is ready, it will open of itself - but first there is a great deal to be done and that must be done patiently and without haste.

—

1972, January 12th

Excerpt of a conversation with Satprem on the name of the twelve outer petals in Mother's symbol:

Do you happen to remember where I wrote the twelve attributes of Mother (the symbol with twelve petals)? There's one, four and twelve.

Satprem: Yes, I think it was for Auroville.

For Auroville? But I said it years ago...

Satprem: I saw it recently.

The twelve?

Sujata goes out in search of the paper.

On this one there aren't any details.

The central circle represents the Divine Consciousness.

The four petals represent the four powers of the Mother.

The twelve petals represent the twelve powers of Mother manifested for Her work.

...

Mother tries to remember the names of the four and the twelve of Her symbol.

(Both the Mother's symbol and the Matrimandir represent a lotus in full bloom.)

In September 1970 Mother issued this message:

"The Matrimandir wants to be the symbol of the Universal Mother according to Sri Aurobindo's teaching." Her symbol and the Matrimandir are symbolic representations of a lotus, which itself symbolises the divine consciousness and, according to Sri Aurobindo: "Mother is the Consciousness and Force of the Divine."

Hence:

The central circle of Her symbol and Matrimandir itself represent the Supreme Mother, the Mahashakti.

The four central petals of Her symbol and Matrimandir's pillars represent Her four Aspects or Personalities.

On 10th November 1954, Mother explained to Her class that the twelve outer petals of Her symbol represent different things: "It signifies anything one wants, you see. 12: that's the number of Aditi, of Mahashakti. So it applies to everything; all Her action has 12 Aspects. There are also Her 12 Virtues, Her 12 Powers, Her 12 Aspects, and then Her 12 Planes of manifestation and many other things that are 12; and the symbol, the number 12 is in itself a symbol. It is the symbol of manifestation, double perfection, in essence and in manifestation, in the creation."

At Matrimandir:

The twelve meditation rooms probably represent Her twelve Virtues.

The twelve gardens may be representing the twelve Powers necessary for Her action.

The "centre" here is Matrimandir's shell, or rather its outer and inner shells. The outside shell is gold (symbolising Divine Truth), while the Inner Chamber is fully white (symbolising the light of Mother, or the Divine Consciousness) and the (double) shell of the sphere will let through a particular type of "Grace Light" (golden-pink).

1972, January 19th

Excerpt of a conversation with Satprem referring to the conversation he had
with Mother on 12th.

Last time I told you I was looking for the twelve attributes (*Mother takes
out a sheet of paper*). Here they are; someone found this:

> Sincérité, Humilité, Gratitude, Persévérance,
> Aspiration, Réceptivité, Progrès, Courage,
> Bonté, Générosité, Egalité, Paix

Sincerity	Humility	Gratitude	Perseverance
Aspiration	Receptivity	Progress	Courage
Kindness	Generosity	Equanimity	Peace

The first eight concern the attitude towards the Divine, and the last four
towards humanity.

And we also found a text from Sri Aurobindo (with a coloured chart of
the twelve petals).

Centre and four powers, white.

The twelve all different colours in three groups: top group red, passing to orange towards yellow; next group, yellow passing through green towards blue; and third group, blue passing through violet towards red. If white is not convenient, the centre may be gold.

Sri Aurobindo, 20 March 1934

The centre is gold.

Satprem: But what did you need these twelve attributes for?

They're going to build twelve rooms around the Matrimandir, at ground level, and Roger wanted each room to have a name: one of the twelve attributes of the Mother, and the corresponding colour.

1972, January 20th

Completion of the excavation. 16,000 work-days; 18,000 to 20,000 m³ of earth have been removed.

10.50 metres deep, 50 metres across (at ground level).

1972, February 21st

The Ceremony marking the beginning of Matrimandir's actual construction.

At 6.15 a.m. with the music of "The Hour of God", the 2,000 well-wishers present there started putting, one by one, a pebble in the concrete mixer.

At 6.45 a.m. Nolini-da read Mother's message for this function which was presided over by 12 persons selected by her.

From left to right: Shyam Sunder, Ramanathan, Prem Malik, Navajata, Charupada, Nolini (standing), Sisir Mitra, Madhav Pandit, Sahana (standing), Nirodbaran, Satprem. Roger Anger (not seen here) is the 12th person, next to Satprem. Barun Tagore is seated behind Charupada.

During this ceremony a piece of fossilised wood was placed at the base of the Mahalakshmi-East pillar to be constructed. On this fossilised wood the Mother inscribed the symbol OM, then wrote the date and "blessings" and her signature.

21 . 12. 72
blessings

Let Auroville be the symbol
of a progressive Unity.
And the best way to realise this is
a unity of aspiration towards the
Divine Perfection in work and in
feeling, in a consecration of the entire life.

1972, February 22nd

Mother's comment to Satprem

All day long on the 21st I had a strong feeling that it was everybody's birthday, and I felt the urge to say "happy birthday" to everyone.

A very strong impression that something new was manifesting in the world, and that all those who were ready and receptive would incarnate it.

In a few days, probably, we will know what it was.

—

1972, February 28th

Message sent by Mother for Auroville's 4th birthday

28th February is Auroville's birthday.

On this day we shall meditate, wherever we are at the designated time, 11:30, with the resolution of working better and of working always more and to open ourselves more and more to the Divine's Will.

Blessings

—

1972, February 29th

The 4th leap-year celebration of the Golden Day of the Supramental Manifestation is celebrated with the concreting of the first layer (a 30cm thick PCC mat) of Matrimandir's foundation.

3. 5. 72.

*Let us all work
with a growing sincerity
for the manifestation
of the Divine Truth.*

With my blessings

Let us all work
with growing sincerity
for the manifestation
of the Divine Truth.
With my blessings

The Mother

1972, June 10th

Letter from Mona Sarkar (SAA) to Mother:

Sweet Mother,

We have completed, for the time being, pouring concrete at the basis of the 4 pillars, on Thursday at night. There was a lot of enthusiasm for going to work at Matrimandir. Work was hard and at times went on throughout the night. Yet it didn't disturb our respective work on the following day. Everything went well except for insignificant incidents. There was a lot of goodwill between us and the people of Auroville, and Mr. Piero was very kind and amiable.

If You have something to tell us or something that didn't go well, tell us directly.

And, despite everything, there was a concrete Presence that made itself felt at Matrimandir.

Pranams
Your child, Mona

Nothing to say except that it is very good

Tenderness and blessings

The Mother

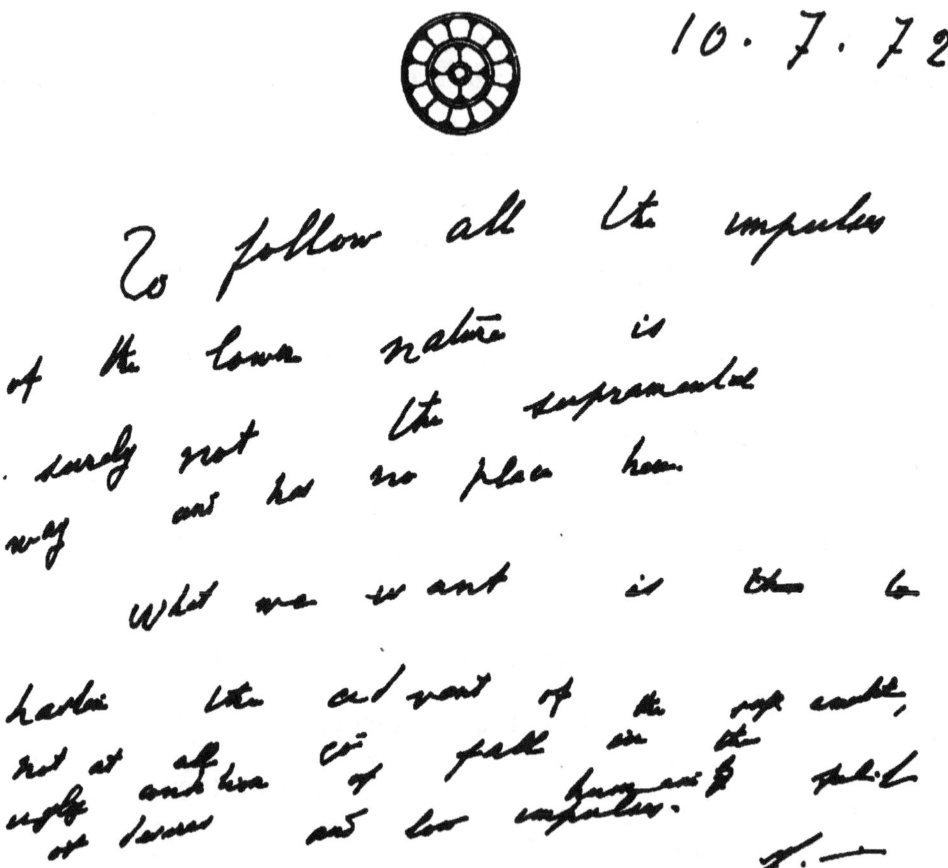

10 . 7 . 72 .

To follow all the impulses
of the lower nature is
surely not the supramental
way and has no place here.

What we want is then to
harbin the old want of the right and left,
not at all here to be filled in the
night of desires and be hungering to fulfil
our lower impulses.

To follow all the impulses

of the lower nature is

surely not the supramental

way and has no place here.

What we want is to

hasten the advent of the supramental,

not at all to fall in the

ugly condition of a humanity full

of desires

and low impulses.

1972, July 17th

Mother writes down the significance of Matrimandir's four pillars for Roger:

North	Mahakali	East	Mahalakshmi
South	Maheshwari	West	Mahasaraswati

Roger notes down Mother's clarification regarding the position and colour of the 12 meditation rooms in the "petals": The colour light blue for Sincerity and dark blue for Peace. Rotating towards the left.

Agreement for this solution.

Maheshwari, Mahakali, Mahalakshmi, Mahasaraswati

Four great Aspects of the Mother, four of her leading Powers and Personalities have stood in front in her guidance of this universe and in her dealings with the terrestrial play. One is her personality of calm wideness and comprehending wisdom and tranquil benignity and inexhaustible compassion and sovereign and surpassing majesty and all-ruling greatness. Another embodies her power of splendid strength and irresistible passion, her warrior mood, her overwhelming will, her impetuous swiftness and world-shaking force. A third is vivid and sweet and wonderful with her deep secret of beauty and harmony and fine rhythm, her intricate and subtle opulence, her compelling attraction and captivating grace. The fourth is equipped with her close and profound capacity of intimate knowledge and careful flawless work and quiet and exact perfection in all things. Wisdom, Strength, Harmony, Perfection are their several attributes and it is these powers that they bring with them into the world, manifest in a human disguise in their Vibhutis and shall found in the divine degree of their ascension in those who can open their earthly nature to the direct and living influence of the Mother. To the four we give the four great names, Maheshwari, Mahakali, Mahalakshmi, Mahasaraswati.

The Mother   Sri Aurobindo

1972, August

Entry in Roger Anger's notes, after a conversation with Mother.

On the subject of the quality of silence at Matrimandir.

I would like people to keep silent. It must be written there (in the Matrimandir area) that one keeps silent, in French, English and Tamil. And no music.

About flowers.

No flowers inside. There should be a room to put them in, in a corridor.

Matrimandir.

In principle not for visitors, reserved for Aurovilians; but not everyone will be admitted. The first condition for those who want to go there is to ask. Those who have contributed to the construction will be admitted in the first place. If there are doubtful cases, they should be referred to me. All those who have a doubtful presence should not go. If there is the slightest doubt, the case should be presented to me. People must be known for their qualifications.

Matrimandir door.

One cannot leave it (the building) open. Then voluntary guardians would be needed, day and night. I think it's simplest with doors.

1972, August 15th: Sri Aurobindo's 100th Birth Anniversary

Excerpt from Ruud Lohman "Matrimandir Diary" (dated Sept. 13th):

On August 15th there was a special midnight meditation to celebrate Sri Aurobindo's Centenary, and a collective meditation at 10:00 a.m. Matrimandir workers were presented with a souvenir poster carrying photographs of Sri Aurobindo, the Mother and the construction team, and Mother's message:

Good will and peace

to all.

Blessings

The Mother

1972, September 14th

Mother agreed that the Aurovilians could carry on with the work. Till then it had only been agreed that they could build the 4 pillars and that a decision on whether to hire a contractor or not would then be taken.

1972, September 20th

Major changes in Matrimandir's design are agreed upon by Roger, Piero and the team of structural engineers from S.E.R.C. – Madras. This is when Matrimandir's Inner Chamber, the dodeca wall and the single pair of spiral ramps became as they are now.

These changes were suggested by Piero to Roger because the structural engineers were finding it too difficult to design structurally the floor of the Chamber.

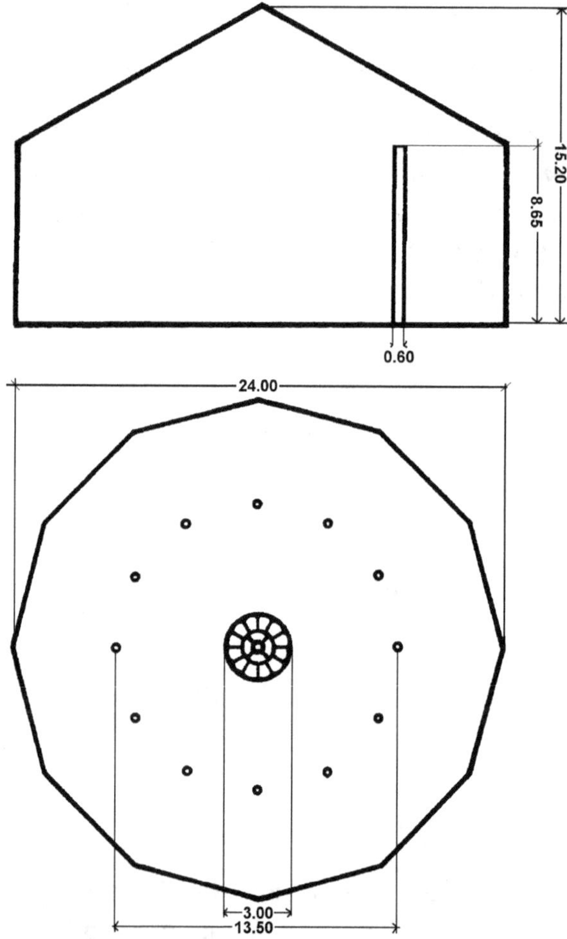

Section and plan of the Inner Chamber

210

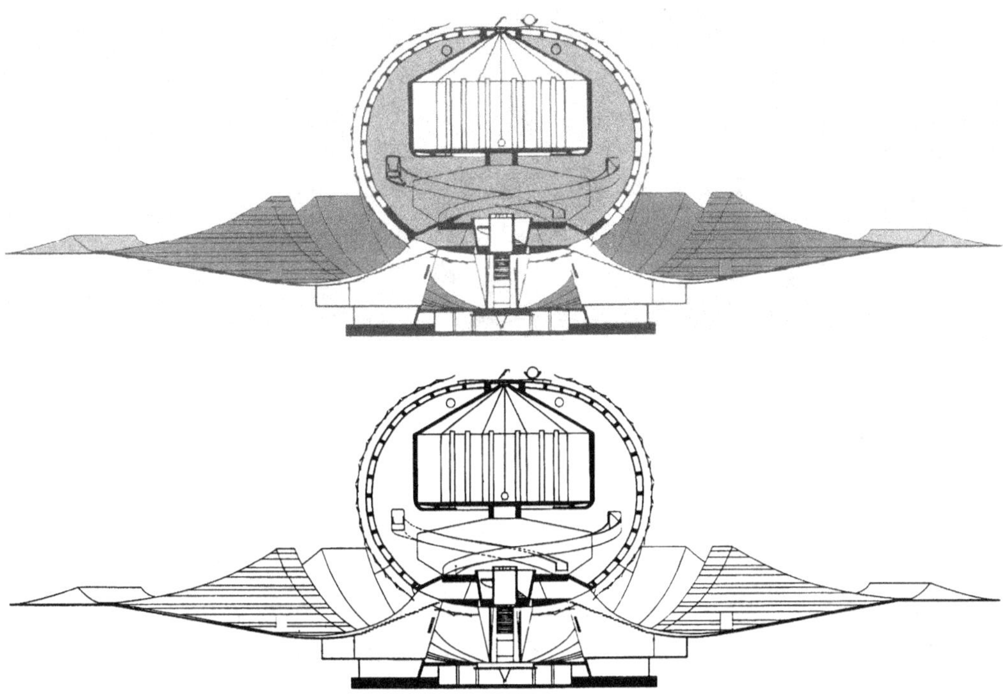

Sphere	36 m dia	Inner Chamber	24 m dia
	29 m height		15.20 m height at centre
Petals	at 6.50 m height extending		8.65 m height of walls
	to a 49 m radius		8.65 m height of columns
Ground level	00 at junction of pillar + first slab		
Foundations	10 m below ground level	Crystal	0.70 m dia

1972, October 20th

Entry in Shyam Sunder's notes:

Day before yesterday when I went to Matrimandir, there came the idea of starting the work of construction of the twelve meditation rooms and the Matrimandir gardens. Mother was happy.

On the other hand we have no money. There is no money to pay for the land already bought, several construction works have stopped; even for the Matrimandir work already done we have borrowed a lakh of Rupees. In spite of this difficulty the idea persists.

Shyam Sunder: I want to know what Mother sees about it.

There is no money at all?
S.S: No, Mother.

I see a pressure in the atmosphere ... but what to do?
S.S: I have spoken to the people at Matrimandir, Piero, Alain. There is the difficulty of money. They have asked me to ask Mother if she says 'yes'. At present, even if one begins, one can begin only slowly.

Are materials necessary?
S.S.: In the beginning, no, it does not cost much. But towards the end, it will cost a good deal.

Mother gave her approval for commencing.
S.S.: Do I say to the people at Matrimandir that Mother has said Yes?
Yes.

Mother gave this message for the concreting of the fourth pillar.

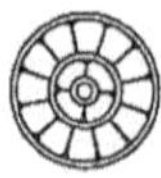

Harmony

Goodwill

Discipline

Truth.

I can work with you only if

you do not say a lie and are at

the service of Truth.

Mahasaraswati - West

Mahakali - North

Mahalakshmi - East

Maheshwari - South

1972, November 5th

Excerpt from Shyam Sunder's notes published in his "Down Memory Lane".

Last evening the four pillars of Matrimandir have been completed. Mother gave a box of toffees for the Matrimandir Camp.

Now that the 4 pillars were complete up to 1st slab level, there was a pause in Matrimandir's construction because there was a need to purchase scaffolding pipes and clamps in order to prop the 1st slab and wood to make its shuttering. Structural design and working drawings needed also to be produced. Ruud Lohman and Alain Grandcolas were very keen to start some other work and asked Mother for permission to start work in the 12 gardens. Soon they decided that, in order to first level the area, it would be better to wait for the arrival of a bulldozer donated by the father of an American Aurovilian. They then got Shyam Sunder's approval to start building the Amphitheatre, which they did in 1973 thanks to working drawings produced by a British-Aurovilian architect, Vikas.

1972, November 24th

At the Matrimandir

6 a.m. 15 minute meditation followed by the commencement of the Matrimandir gardens work.

Blessings

1972, December 5th

Excerpt from Ruud Lohman's "Matrimandir Diary":

Nature celebrates the Mahasamadhi of Sri Aurobindo today with heavy storms and much rain. Not a single worker has shown up and it looks as if it will be a quiet day around here.

The cyclone which it was predicted would pass over Pondicherry at midnight has not touched upon Matrimandir. The Centenary Year is drawing to a close. For Matrimandir it was the year of the pillars: on the first Darshan day of this year, February 21st, we had an official function with a symbolic commencement of the concreting; on the last Darshan day we meditated at 6:00 a.m. between the completed pillars.

Very broadly we may say that the three chapters indicated above (conception, excavation, pillars) each covered a year. The Conception and Preparation started at the end of the 60's and set the tone for 1970. The excavation was executed in 1971; the pillars with their footings in 1972. 1973 will be the year of the lower half of the sphere, beginning maybe with February Darshan or, more likely, with April Darshan. By then the Amphitheatre may be completed.

Most people around here expect the whole project to be ready by the end of 1977, just before Mother's Centenary on February 21st, 1978.

Excerpt from Roger Toll's diary:

Mahasamadhi Day, 22nd anniversary of Sri Aurobindo's death. Mother had said the day should be dedicated to contemplate the meaning of death. Group meditation at 10 in the meditation room of the Camp. Beautiful atmosphere, togetherness. The rain and wind are increasing, and we learn of coming cyclone with 150 kph winds. All day it builds, winds very strong with much rain. Everything gets damp and uncomfortable. No food arrives, no transportation, can't go out in the storm. Then the electricity goes. I sleep early, then awake at 11:30 to enormous wind and driving rain. Trees being uprooted, tremendous air pressure. The bamboo structure of my new hut is shaking wildly, and I retreat to Seyril's room.

—

Awake to much damage, but nothing serious, only minor hardship, everything damp, little food and still no electricity to run the pump for water. During the bad part of the storm after midnight, everyone seemed to be awake, praying and concentrating. We make repairs to the Matrimandir sheds. I repair my roof, have good talks with friends. We hear there will be no electricity for at least a week, which means problems for bathing, cooking meals, flushing toilets.

1972, December 8th

Excerpt from Ruud Lohman's "Matrimandir Diary":

The cyclone, which did not make it for Sri Aurobindo's Mahasamadhi day, arrived the next day. The whole night after the 5th it blew, at a velocity approximating 150 km/h. Pondy, being right on the coast, suffered quite a lot: many trees were uprooted and even the big Service tree at Sri Aurobindo's Samadhi lost one of its biggest branches. Mother never liked our constructing dwellings in keet and bamboo in Auroville; the monsoon did not like it either and blew down a lot of them. Forecomers was almost wiped out; we lost the community kitchen in Aspiration, the temporary Health Centre and the Gymnasium. Matrimandir was one of the places that suffered least. The structure of the Workers' Camp, temporary though it is, made it right through; it only grumbled and trembled. At the construction site the carpentry workshop which was only half completed came down, that's about all. Of course, there was some damage to the roofs of all other buildings, but that is in the nature of things. The Matrimandir Gardens' Nursery was hit quite hard. Some huge mango trees fell right down and cannot be saved. All around Pondy and Auroville, and also right in our own Workers' Camp garden, all the Transformation trees were lost. Madhav Pandit asked Narad yesterday to look for whatever Transformation' flowers he could find around here and send them daily to Mother, who seems to give out many of them each day. We heard that Mother had told Satprem that the cyclone was able to come because the level of consciousness has gone down so much.

The pillars look beautiful these days, since they stand with their feet in the reddish water, more water than we have ever seen inside. Of course, the cyclone disrupted all the electricity supply in the surrounding area, so we cannot pump it out.

The urn has become an island floating in the projected amphitheatre; in order to measure circles and segments we have to wade into the muddy water almost up to our waists. The excavation on the stage area had already started before the monsoon, but now we cannot even think of working there.

So this morning when the workers came, we had to start something new again. Nowadays almost every day we have a new beginning of something. Vikas is working full-time on the drawings for the amphitheatre and complained, "We need three teams of international architects to keep up with Alain's excavation impetus". Anyhow, recently it was decided that at the rear of the amphitheatre an underground control room and many toilets would be built. This morning we started the excavation for it after roughly measuring the site yesterday. At 6:52 a.m. Alain, Tom and I drove in unison the first three shovels into the soft red earth. It really looks out of time and place to stand there with lots of muddy earth clinging to your bare feet in the wide stretch of land where not a trace of civilisation is visible, much less the City of the Future, and talk about plugs for video recording, control panels and loud speaker systems.

The twelve petals surrounding the sphere of Matrimandir seem to create technical problems. Amusing that very often in discussions between technical-minded people, cost is mentioned and the need to find the cheapest solution. As if in this whole strange, divine, irrational, supramental venture called Auroville a few millions of Rupees or Dollars played any role. We don't have a paise now but still we go on constructing. To speak in terms of holding down the cost of the Soul of Auroville is as odd as talking about the golden discs, all the marble which will be needed and, after all, the whole project.

This morning an engineer came who was invited to take charge of the construction of the petals with meditation rooms, one Mr. Nagarshet, who retired from Government service and joined the Ashram. In a meeting with Piero, Ramanathan, Vikas, Alain and myself, the three possible solutions for the petals were discussed once again. First, the petals could be hollow, but this creates huge problems, regarding scaffolding. Roger, in last week's meeting, said he does not like this solution very much because it is not 'true', not a real symbol of the earth breaking open to give birth, etc. Piero prefers this solution for technical reasons because it does not pose the problem of the tremendous pressure of earth against the 17-metre high sidewalls. To have the meditation rooms inside and leave the remainder of the space open and unused seems, however, artificial. Then it might be better to use the whole area inside the petals as meditation rooms.

Second solution: to build the rooms, fill up the whole thing with earth, and then construct the shell of the petals against the earth. This seems to be the easier and more-natural solution. A third solution is not really a solution at all but rather an attempt to avoid a lot of trouble and expense: to fill up the petals without having meditation rooms at all.

The procedure for coming to a decision will be as follows: three groups will make a preliminary study of each of the alternatives to come to the best and 'most economic' solution. One group, to whom the scheme has already been proposed, is the Structural Engineering Research Centre in Madras (SERC), which has been working for about a year on the sphere of Matrimandir. A second group would be Mr. Nagarshet and his engineering friends in Bombay. Names were mentioned for a third group of individuals. A time limit would be fixed, after which the three parties would sit together with us here to discuss and take a final decision. The one whose suggestions appeal best will be asked to work out the details.

Ruud Lohman wrote on 9.12.1972 in his Matrimandir diary:

When we start constructing the four ribs of the main structure we must know of what material the shell will be made. We always thought it would be of concrete and the engineering research team in Madras has calculated everything, down to the foundations, on that supposition. About two months ago Roger was studying Matrimandir again and he came to the conclusion that there are other ways of making skins for Matrimandir. One way would be to attach a steel frame to the ribs, in triangles or any other form, and to cover it over with some translucent, opaque or other material. He had in mind a solution which, he told us, had been used for storing war materials, the so-called cocoon, some sort of polyester that can be sprayed onto any object to make it waterproof and totally sealed. On his latest trip to France he gathered some more information on the cocoon and came back with a few pieces and advertisements. Before he left again, the team in Madras was informed of possible changes in the structure, which could upset all their previous calculations on which they have spent the greater part of this year. Concrete or cocoon was the issue for several weeks. Yesterday, Roger and Piero met and, it seems, they came to a whole new solution about which we'll be hearing more soon. It is something like concrete rings with open spaces in between which will filter the light into the sphere. Attached to the rings there will be a sort of concrete channel which will conduct the rainwater to a central canal so that it does not pour down in streams as it does from an umbrella. The golden discs will then be attached to the concrete rings. It is a kind of in-between solution: the strength and solemnity of concrete coupled with the translucency of other materials Roger has had in mind for some time.

We may have to go through many more solutions and suggestions, however, before futuristic beauty is obtained.

It is probably during Roger's next visit that Mother will give him a small piece of a saree to show him the colour of Matrimandir's inner skin. (It is the colour of the hibiscus she had named "Auroville" and "beauty of supramental love", Her comment for this flower being: "It invites us to live at its height.")

On 11.7.1970, Mother had spoken to Satprem about this particular light, while talking about the Tamil Yogi, Swami Ramalingam:

Excerpt from a conversation with Satprem about "Grace light":

Satprem: Sweet Mother, one last thing, Rod asked a question: he asks if that vast "Grace-Light" or "Truth-Light" (of which Swami Ramalingam, 1823 – 1874, who lived near Chidambaram speaks) is the supramental light?

Which light?

Satprem: That vast "Grace-Light."

Grace-Light... Oh! I liked that very much in his letter... Grace-Light. That's what is at work, you know: the work that is being done through this (the body) is precisely like that, it's just like a "Grace-Light". That pleased me very much. It's just like that.

You know, it's a light that has several degrees, and in the most material it's slightly... this must be the supramental force because it is slightly golden, slightly pink (you know this light), but very very pale. There's one

229

(gesture indicating another, higher layer) that is white like milk, opaque – it is very strong. And there is one (gesture very high) which is a shade of white... which is of a transparent light. That one is something curious: one drop of that on the hostile forces dissolves them. They melt like that (gesture meaning "in no time at all"). I told all that to Sri Aurobindo, he confirmed it completely to me.

That is essentially the Grace in its... (gesture very high) supreme state. It's a Light... it is colourless, you know, it's transparent, and that light (I have experienced it, I am speaking of it because I know it): you put it on a hostile being and... It melts just like that. It's extraordinary.... And then, in its guise of what you could call "benevolent" (that is, the Grace that succours and helps and cures), it's as white as milk. And if I want an entirely material action (but this is recent, it's recently, since that new Consciousness came), then in its physical action, on the physical, it becomes slightly coloured: it's luminous, it's gold with pink in it, but it's not pink... (Mother picks up a hibiscus near her). It's like that.

Satprem: Like the "Auroville" flower?

Like the Auroville flower. But I DELIBERATELY chose it as the Auroville flower because of that. And I have the impression that that's the supramental colour: when I see beings of the supramental, they are... not exactly this colour... It's not like a flower, it's like flesh. But it's like that (Mother indicates the colour of the flower).

"Beauty of Supramental Love"

1973

When you are conscious
of the whole world at the
same time, then you can
become conscious of the Divine.

Au-dessus de la conscience
Au-delà de la parole
O Toi, Suprême Conscience
Unique Réalité
Vérité divine.

Beyond man's consciousness
Beyond speech
O Thou, Supreme Consciousness
Unique Reality
Divine Truth

The Mother

Mother's Balcony Darshan, on 21st February 1973 ▶

Mother's last message for Auroville.

27.3.73

Auroville is created to
realise the ideal of Sri Aurobindo
who taught us the Karma
yoga. Auroville is for those who
want to do the yoga of work.
To live in Auroville
means to do the yoga
of work. So all Aurovilians
must take up a work and
do it as yoga.

Blessings

The Mother

1973, May

1973, November 11th - 14th

The non-continuous concreting of the first level started on 11th at 3:30 pm and ended on 14th at 6:20 am.

The non-continuous concreting of the 8 small tip-ends of the 4 twin pillars (which rise above the first level) started on 15th and was completed on 17th November at 7:25 pm − that is, exactly when Mother left her body. Mother had named these 4 pillars after the 4 Aspects or Personalities of the Universal Mother: Mahalaksmi (East), Mahakali (North), Mahasaraswati (West), Maheshwari (South).

1973, November 15th, 16th, 17th

Excerpt from Ruud Lohman's Matrimandir diary
dated 29th December:

On November 15th, 16th and 17th concreting of the last summit portion of the pillars above slab level 1 continued.

The entire work was finished on 17th November, precisely between 7:07 and 7:25 p.m.

When information came to the Matrimandir Camp that the Mother had left her body, it was seen that all the pillars of the Matrimandir had been completed by, and simultaneously, with the time of her physical withdrawal.

This monumental work, needing clear weather, proceeded for six days during ▶ the monsoon season. It was completed at the West pillar summit at 7.25 p.m. on 17th November during perfect weather. When information came to Matrimandir workers on Sunday morning of 18th November that The Mother had left Her body at 7:25 p.m. on November 17th, it was seen that all four pillars of the Matrimandir had been completed exactly at the time of Her physical withdrawal.

1973 was the year of Mother's physical withdrawal. In May she stopped receiving people, even her secretaries.

On November 17th she left her body – exactly at the time when Matrimandir's four pillars were completed (which required casting the 1st level slab). She had named the four pillars after the four Powers / Personalities of the Universal Mother.

The 4 pillars were completed after the removal of the shuttering of their tips, ▶ whose concreting ended on 17th November.

Matrimandir - The Soul of Auroville

The Matrimandir, lit up at night, looks like some strange ship in the desert, an ark under construction, symbol of a new and dawning age. The Mother called the Matrimandir "the cohesive force of Auroville"; "a symbol of the Divine's answer to man's aspiration for perfection," and "the soul of Auroville."

This binding force that guides and upholds Auroville in a powerful if indefinable way was tangible and evident at a 19-hour concreting of a dome platform for the roof of the structure, held at Matrimandir on 2-3 June 1988. Over sixty Aurovilians, adults, children, Westerners and Indians alike, worked through the night as a concrete mixer ground out its load of sand, cement and stones, which was lifted, one wheelbarrow at a time, by a crane to the top of the structure, to then be poured and vibrated into the mould of reinforced steel and plywood shuttering, completed after months of work a few days before. From within the inner chamber, where scaffolding rises in an Escher-like configuration to the sloping roof, the hum of vibrators on the roof above resounded, echoing like the low chanting of Buddhist monks.

Roger Harris, 1988

Champaklal working at the Matrimandir ▶

2008

Do not look behind, look always in front,
at what you want to do —
and you are sure of progressing.

Arrival of the Crystal globe in 1991

2008 was the year when the Matrimandir construction was completed.

Chronology of the construction works

1973 - 1976 : Concrete structure up to the top ring joining the 4 ribs.

1976 - 1978 : Concrete structure of the Inner Chamber.

1978 - 1988 : Ramps and space frame of the sphere of Matrimandir. Construction of the crane and its installation on top of Matrimandir.

1991 : The Chamber started to be used for meditation after the installation of the 12 columns and the Crystal globe on 22nd August 1991. The final cube-stand was installed later.

1994 : The carpet was installed in February 1994. Completion of the Inner Chamber.

1991 - 1999 : Fabrication and installation of the ferrocement outer skin of Matrimandir. Construction of the 12 petals around Matrimandir.

1997 - 2002 : Fabrication of the 1,400 golden discs for the outer skin.

2000 - 2006 : Completion of the layout and cladding of the radial paths, the general contouring of the gardens and the Lotus pond below Matrimandir. Installation of the automated irrigation system for the whole gardens area.

2006 - 2011 : Construction of the Garden of Unity near the Banyan tree and of the first of the 12 gardens: the Garden of Existence. Beginning of the construction of the Gardens of Consciousness and Bliss.

2007 : The holes for the influx of chilled air in the Chamber's ceiling were modified.

2002 - 2007 : Completion of the inner skin triangles and outer skin with golden discs; finishing of the marble cladding inside the Matrimandir and installation of the two glass parapets on the two ramps.

2008 - 2013 : Construction of Unity Garden, building the mini amphitheatre with its fountain.

2008 : Completion of the Matrimandir on 21.2.2008 of the 12 petals and the main radial pathways of its gardens.

2009 : April 16th - start of the Garden of Existence.

2010 : January - start of the Garden of Consciousness.

2012 : Start of Garden of Bliss.

2012 - 2015 : Completion of the Unity Garden, with its fountain, the Garden of Consciousness with its cascade and the near completion of the Garden of Bliss. Creation of six mini test ponds as studies for the future Matrimandir lake.

2017 : January - start of the Garden of Progress.

2019 : February 21 - start of the Garden of the Unexpected.

2020 : Completion of the Unexpected Garden.

The Matrimandir and the Mother's Symbol

The Matrimandir wants to be the symbol of the Universal Mother according to Sri Aurobindo's teaching.

The Mother

The Mother's symbol

Both the Mother's symbol and the Matrimandir represent a lotus in full bloom.

The centre of the Mother's symbol and the Matrimandir itself represent the Divine Consciousness, the Supreme Mother, the Mahashakti.

The 4 petals of the Mother's symbol and the four pillars which support Matrimandir represent the four Aspects or Personalities of the Mother: Maheshwari Wisdom, Mahalakshmi Harmony, Mahakali Strength and Mahasaraswati Perfection.

The 12 petals of the Mother's symbol represent the 12 'pearls' Mme Théon (wife of the Mother's instructor in occultism) was the first to 'see' above her head and made her affirm: *"You are that (the Mother) because you have this (12 'pearls') over your head. Only that can have this!"* Mother explained further to her class in 1954:

(The 12 'petals') signifies anything one wants, you see, 12: that's the number of Aditi, of Mahashakti. So it applies to everything; all Her action has 12 aspects. There are also Her 12 Virtues, Her 12 Powers, Her 12 Aspects, and then Her 12 Planes of manifestation and many other things that are 12; and the symbol, the number 12 is in itself a symbol. It is the symbol of manifestation, double perfection, in essence and in manifestation, in the creation.

The Mother

This 12 is represented in many different ways at the Matrimandir, among which: Mother named the 12 meditation rooms inside the Matrimandir's 12 large 'petals': *Sincerity, Humility, Gratitude, Perseverance, Aspiration, Receptivity, Progress, Courage, Kindness, Generosity, Equality, Peace.* They seem to represent the Mother's 12 '*Virtues*' or '*Qualities*'.

She named the 12 Gardens around the Matrimandir: *Existence, Consciousness, Bliss, Light, Life, Power, Wealth, Usefulness, Progress, Youth, Harmony, Perfection.* They seem to represent what she calls "*the twelve powers of the Mother manifested for Her work*"; and Sri Aurobindo wrote that these "*twelve powers are the vibrations that are necessary for the complete manifestation.*"

The Matrimandir's four entrances

In 1972, Mother named the four pairs of pillars which support the Matrimandir after Her four Aspects or Personalities. These pillars serve also as the four main entrances to the sphere. In Sri Aurobindo's words, these Personalities are:

Maheshwari

One is her personality of calm wideness and comprehending wisdom and tranquil benignity and inexhaustible compassion and sovereign and surpassing majesty and all-ruling greatness.

Mahakali

Another embodies her power of splendid strength and irresistible passion, her warrior mood, her overwhelming will, her impetuous swiftness and world-shaking force.

Mahalakshmi

A third is vivid and sweet and wonderful with her deep secret of beauty and harmony and fine rhythm, her intricate and subtle opulence, her compelling attraction and captivating grace.

Mahasaraswati

The fourth is equipped with her close and profound capacity to initiate knowledge and careful flawless work and quiet and exact perfection in all things.

North entrance to the Matrimandir

Above, on the sides and behind each entrance (between pillars), a golden 'shield' has been installed to mark the Matrimandir's four entrances, and in front of these 'shields' has also been placed a very large golden disc with four petals, at the centre of which a geometrical shape indicates which entrance one faces:

North	Mahakali	Strength	Red square
South	Maheshwari	Wisdom	Orange hexagon
East	Mahalakshmi	Harmony	Pink circle
West	Mahasaraswati	Perfection	Light blue triangle

This mantra is written in golden letters in two places at the second level of the Matrimandir:

A mantra to the Universal Mother written in Sanskrit by Sri Aurobindo.

The first three words of its English transliteration were also written by Sri Aurobindo - and the last two by The Mother as He had written them. Its English translation is by The Mother.

Inner Chamber

The Inner Chamber has been built exactly according to the vision of the Mother.

She described it to an Ashram engineer, Udar, who at her request made a measured drawing which she then passed on to the architect. She told him not to change anything and to include this Chamber in a larger building, which she said she had not 'seen'.

The Inner Chamber has a 12m radius (wall included). Its floor is covered with a white woollen carpet (except at the centre).

Its wall is 8.65 m. high. It has 12 facets which represent "the 12 months of the year" and are clad with white marble from Lasa, Italy.

Section and plan of the Inner Chamber:

Its white ceiling also has 12 facets, each one resting on one of the wall's facets and sloping by 30° upwards towards the centre. The Chamber's height at its centre is thus 15.2 m.

It has two double doors (located on opposite sides) made of thick white marble slabs. As wished by the Mother, the entrance door faces East. When closed, these doors are more or less invisible as she did not 'see' them in her vision.

It has 12 large steel cylindrical columns of 60cm diameter, covered with white lacquer, which the Mother had clearly 'seen' and which stand half-way between the centre of the room and each one of its 12 corners.

As their height is the same as that of the walls, they do not touch the ceiling and have no structural function.

As it has no windows, it is air-conditioned. The only light comes from a vertical beam of light, which the Mother wanted to be slightly golden and visible. This beam is normally a ray of the sun which is reflected down into the Chamber by a heliostat whose computerised tracking system keeps it very precisely oriented. Electrical spotlights create a similar effect at night and on cloudy days.

At the centre of the room, there is the object of concentration upon which falls a single vertical beam of sunlight.

This object is a crystal globe (70cm diameter, 400kg) custom-made of optically perfect glass in Germany by 'Schott' and later polished by 'Zeiss'.

It rests on a 'cube stand' (35cm side) consisting of 4 upright gilded symbols of Sri Aurobindo that hold each other up by the points of their triangles.

This 'cube' stands at the centre of the room on a 3m diameter symbol of the Mother, which is engraved in a white marble slab.

The crystal globe is positioned exactly at the flattened sphere's centre.

The Mother stressed that "the important thing is the play of the sunbeam on the centre. Because that becomes a symbol – the symbol of the future realisation."

The Inner Chamber is a place meant for concentration, to "learn how to concentrate" with a view to try to finding one's consciousness.

Sri Aurobindo on Religions

Concentration, for our yoga, means when the consciousness is fixed in a particular state (e.g. peace) or movement (e.g. aspiration, will, coming into contact with the Mother, taking the Mother's name); meditation is when the inner mind is looking at things to get the right knowledge.

I must say that it is far from my purpose to propagate any new religion, new or old, for humanity in the future. A way to be opened that is still blocked, not a religion to be founded, is my conception of the matter.

Letters on Yoga, p. 139

The Mother clearly expressed the wish that Sri Aurobindo's and her teaching should not become the basis of any new religion or sect. Hence, she did not want religious practices and rituals of any kind to take place in the Matrimandir – not even organised collective concentrations. No ritual, no meditation guide, no statues, no photos, no incense, no flowers, no music, nothing that might give birth to a new cult.

Area below the Matrimandir

Below the Matrimandir, the architect initially wanted to build a lotus pond, but when he realised that lotuses will not bloom in the shade, instead of plants, he used 216 petal-shaped marble slabs to create a pond over which water flows from the outside towards the centre. At the centre of this pond, there is a crystal globe (17cm dia.) which will receive the beam of sunlight which permeates Matrimandir from top to bottom, as if to illumine the depths.

Arrangements have been made to enable people to concentrate on the Mother's four *Aspects* or *Personalities* while sitting under the pair of pillars which she named after these. Above the lotus pond, a symbol of the Mother clad in white marble allows the sunbeam to pass through its central point and fall onto the small crystal globe.

Roger Anger's final plan for the Matrimandir Lake

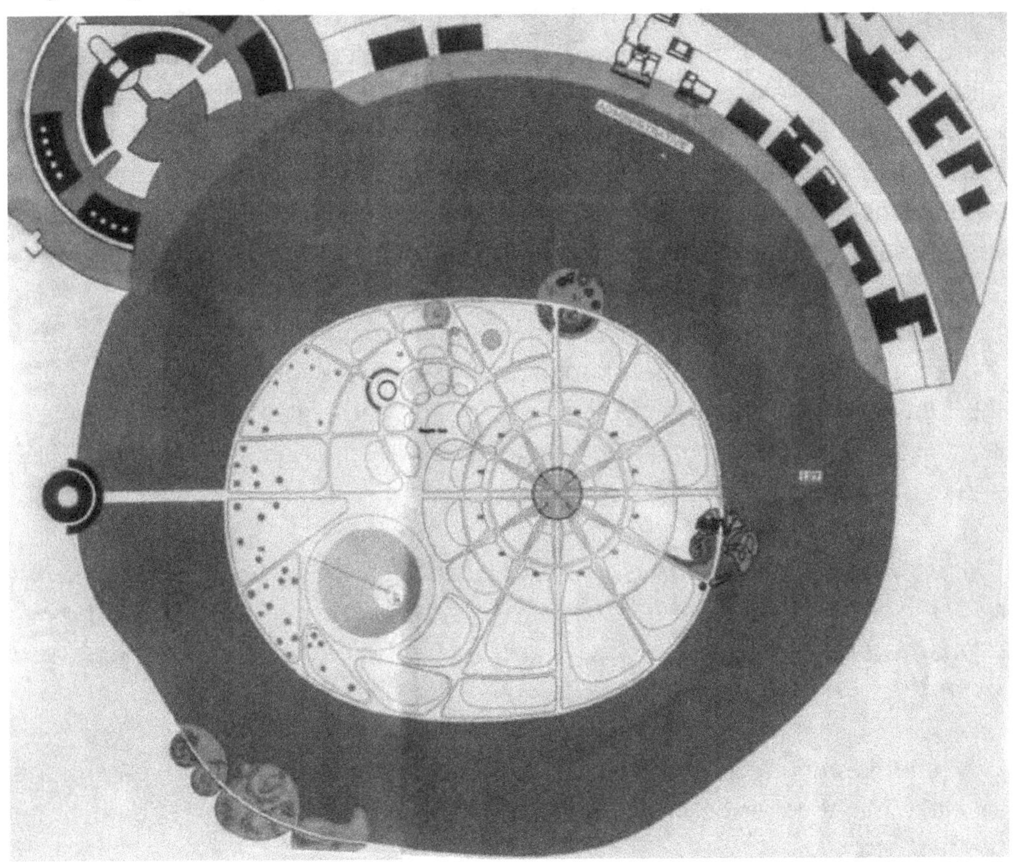

Future Lake & Water Supply

Though she was fully aware of the area's difficult water situation, from the outset Mother said that Matrimandir and its twelve gardens would be surrounded by a lake. She envisaged different solutions to provide water for the future town and lake: she repeatedly mentioned the possibility of desalinating seawater and even spoke of using water from the Himalayas; but when an Aurovilian hydro-geologist explained to her that as long as average rainfalls would remain abundant here (1,300 mm/year), the problem was one of adequate resource management and not one of insufficient resources, she concluded:

"The Aurovilians will have to use their ingenuity to solve this problem."

Her architect, Roger Anger, kept stressing that "the lake", as pointed out by the Mother, "was meant to be a source of drinking water for the residents of Auroville and for irrigation of the lands of Auroville." Indeed, in December 1969, she told Satprem:

"Roger had an idea, it's an island at the centre, with water around, running water which will be used for the whole water supply of the city; and when it has flowed through the city, it will be sent to a (treatment) plant, and from there to irrigate all the cultivated lands around."

Mother kept on reassuring Huta, a lady close to her who kept worrying that this lake might never be created, that it would be there and, in 1970, she sent her this note:

"It has been decided and remains decided that the Matrimandir will be surrounded with water. However, water is not available just now and will be available only later; so it is decided to build the Matrimandir now and surround it with water only later; perhaps in a few years' time... The Matrimandir will be built now and water brought round it later."

The future island's shape and size were finalised early in 1971 (and hence the location of the lake's inner bank) when Mother approved Roger Anger's model of the island whose shape is an oval of the same proportions as that of Matrimandir's vertical section but 10 times larger (360m x 290m). She commented that "10 is the number of accomplishment".

Galaxy model

Photo Credits

Most of the photographs in this book are from
the collection of Auroville Archives and the
Sri Aurobindo Ashram Archives

Barun Tagore, Page 41

Dominique Darr, Pages 57, 134, 152, 153, 155, 156, 158, 176,
185, 186, 187

Venkatesh, Page 188

Gilbert Gaucher, Page 150

Roger Toll, Pages 197, 200, 211, 213, 214, 215, 216, 234

Indra Poddar, Pages 134, 152, 153, 191, 192, 199, 233, 239, 241

Achim Brockhaus, Page 237

Franz Fassbender, Pages, 251, 259, 265 & Cover photo

Building Matrimandir

1972 – 2008

Auroville Video Productions
presents

How it all began.....

SCAN QR CODE
TO WATCH THE FILM

International Publications

Auroville Architecture
by Franz Fassbender

Auroville Form Style and Design
by Franz Fassbender

Landscapes and Gardens of Auroville
by Franz Fassbender

Inauguration of Auroville
by Franz Fassbender

Auroville in a Nutshell
by Tim Wrey

Death doesn't exist
The Mother on Death, Sri Aurobindo on Rebirth
Compiled by Franz Fassbender

Divine Love
Compiled by Franz Fassbender

Five Dream
by Sri Aurobindo

A Vision
Compiled by Franz Fassbender

Passage to More than India
by Dick Batstone

The Mother on Japan
Compiled by Franz Fassbender

Children of Change: A Spiritual Pilgrimage
by Amrit (Howard Shoji Iriyama)

Memories of Auroville - told by early Aurovilians
by Janet Feran

The Journeying Years
by Dianna Bowler

Auroville Reflected
by Bindu Mohanty

Finding the Psychic Being
by Loretta Shartsis

The Teachings of Flowers
The Life and Work of the Mother of the Sri Aurobindo
Ashram
by Loretta Shartsis

The Supramental Transformation
by Loretta Shartsis

**The Mother's Yoga - 1956-1973 (English & French)
Vol. 1, 1956-1967 & Vol. 2, 1968-1973**
by Loretta Shartsis

Antithesis of Yoga
by Jocelyn Janaka

Bougainvilleas PROTECTION
by Narad (Richard Eggenberger), Nilisha Mehta

Crossroad The New Humanity
by Paulette Hadnagy

Die Praxis Des Integralen Yoga
by M. P. Pandit

The Way of the Sunlit Path
by William Sullivan

Wildlife great and small of India's Coromandel
by Tim Wrey

A New Education With A Soul
by Marguerite Smithwhite

Featured Titles

Divine Love

The texts presented in this book are selected from the Mother and Sri Aurobindo.
"Awakened to the meaning of my heart. That to feel love and oneness is to live. And this the magic of our golden change, is all the truth I know or seek, O sage."

Sri Aurobindo, Savitri, Book XII, Epilog

A Vision by the Mother

On 28th May 1958, the Mother recounted a vision she once had of a wonderful Being of Love and Consciousness, emanated from the Supreme Origin and projected directly into the Inconscient so that the creation would gradually awaken to the Supramental Consciousness. The Mother's account of this vision was brought out a first time in November 1906, in the Revue Cosmique, a monthly review published in Paris.

A Dream – Aims and Ideals of Auroville
the Mother on Auroville

50 years of Auroville from 28.02.1968 - 28.02.2018
Today, information about Auroville is abundant. Many people try to make meaning out of Auroville – about its conception, to what direction should we grow towards, and, what are we doing here?

But what was Mother's original Dream and what was her Vision for Auroville back then?

Matrimandir Talks by the Mother

This book presents most of Mother's Matrimandir talks, including how she conceived the idea for this special concentration and meditation building in Auroville.

Memories of Auroville - Told by early Aurovilians

Memories of Auroville is a book about the very early days of Auroville based on interviews made in 1997 with Aurovilians who lived here between 1968 and 1973. The interviews presented in this book are part of a history program for newcomers that I had created with my friend, Philip Melville in 1997. The plan was to divide Auroville's history into different eras and then interview Aurovilians according to their area of knowledge. Our first section would cover the years from 1968 till 1973 when the Mother was still in her physical body.

The Way of the Sunlit Path

May The Way of the Sunlit Path be a convenient guide for activating this ancient truth as a support for a Conscious Evolution.
May it illumine the transformation offered to us in the Integral Yoga.

A Dream Takes Shape (in English, French, Hindi)

A comprehensive brochure on the international township of Auroville in, ranging from its Charter and "Why Auroville?" to the plan of the township, the central Matrimandir, the national pavilions and residences, to working groups, the economy, making visits, how to join, its relationship to the Sri Aurobindo Ashram, and its key role in the future of the world. This brochure endeavours to highlight how The Mother envisioned Auroville from its inception, some of the major achievements realised over the years, and some of the currently faced in implementing the guidelines which she gave.

Mother on Japan

I had everything to learn in Japan. For four years, from an artistic point of view, I lived from wonder to wonder. And everything in this city, in this country, from beginning to end, gives you the impression of impermanence, of the unexpected, the exceptional... ...everything in this city, in this country, from beginning to end, gives you the impression of impermanence, of the unexpected, the exceptional. You always come to things you did not expect, you want to find them again and they are lost – they have made something else which is equally charming.

Auroville Reflected

On 28 February 1968, on an impoverished plateau on the Coromandel Coast of South India, about 4,000 people from around the world gathered for a most unusual inauguration. Handfuls of soil from the countries of the world were mixed together as a symbol of human unity. Why did Indira Gandhi, the erstwhile Prime Minister of India, support this development for "a city the earth needs?" Why did UNESCO endorse this project? Why does the Dalai Lama continue to be involved in the project? What led anthropologist Margaret Mead to insist that records must be kept of its progress? Why did both historian William Irwin Thompson and United Nations representative Robert Muller note that this social experiment may be a breakthrough for humanity even as critics commented, "it is an impossible dream"?

A House For the Third Millennium

Essays on Matrimandir

Nightwatch at the Matrimandir...
A cosmic spectacle; the black expanse above, the big black crater of Matrimandir's excavation carved deep into the soil. The four pillars - two of which are completed and the other two nearing completion - are four huge ships coming together from the four corners of the earth to meet at this pro propitious spot...

Passage to More than India

This book is a voyage of discovery. In 1959 the author, Dick Batstone, a classically educated bookseller in England, with a Christian background, comes across a life of the great Indian polymath Sri Aurobindo, though a series of apparently fortuitous circumstances. A meeting in Durham, England, leads him to a determination to get to the Sri Aurobindo Ashram in Pondicherry, a former French territory south of Madras.

www.ingramcontent.com/pod-product-compliance
Lightning Source LLC
LaVergne TN
LVHW081303210726
843509LV00019B/202